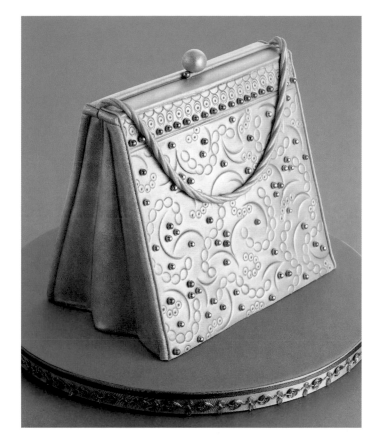

QUICK AND CLEVER

party
cakes

QUICK AND CLEVER

party cakes

Lindy Smith

MEREHURST

Contents

To my sister Lucy, without whose help this book would never have been completed in time. Thanks Lu.

Introduction

Stuck for inspiration? I hope that by looking at the range of contemporary and fun cake designs included in this book, you will find something in these pages that says 'make me!'.

Many of the cakes are designs that I have created for my own children who, as you can probably imagine, ask for all sorts of things. Do not be deceived – despite appearances, many of the cakes are very easy to make and the optional painting stage can often be omitted if this seems daunting or if time is short.

To help you plan ahead, I have broken up the decorating into stages. One of the secrets of successful cakes is to make and decorate a cake over a few days so that each stage has a chance to dry. If possible, try to complete the stages on different days as this will make everything a lot easier and saves time in the long run.

If, on the other hand, you need a cake in a hurry, I have suggested various short cuts to reduce the time spent decorating each cake.

No matter what time you have available, I hope you will agree that making and decorating a special cake for someone is worth every minute!

Have fun and enjoy!

Lindy

Equipment

With each cake, I have listed the equipment needed and given alternatives wherever possible. You don't need to invest in a huge number of tools, but there are a few invaluable ones, such as a sugar shaper, that will give you excellent results and save you time.

1 **Baking tins** Round and square tins, plus a multisize, adjustable pan.

2 **Sugar shaker** Sprinkle icing sugar on a surface to stop sugarpaste sticking.

3 **Spacers** For rolling out paste. These can easily be home made.

4 **Palette** For mixing paste food colours together prior to any painting stages.

5 **Large rolling pin** For rolling out sugarpaste to cover a cake.

6 **Brush (for texturing)** To create texture e.g. on Harvest Tractor cake.

7 **Natural sponge** Used for graded, textured paint effects.

8 **Non-stick work board** Used for rolling out modelling paste and pastillage.

9 **Small rolling pin** For rolling out modelling paste and pastillage.

10 **Drinking straw** Used to make patterns e.g. on Party Bag cake.

11 **Smoother** Helps to create a really smooth and even finish to sugarpaste.

12 **Carving knife** Essential for shaping the cakes prior to decorating them.

13 **Palette knife** Used for scoring and cutting sugarpaste.

14 **Set square** Helps to check vertical lines e.g. on Party Bag cake.

15 **Paintbrushes** A range of sizes is useful for painting and adding shine to cakes.

16 **Sugar shaper** Creates pieces of shaped sugarpaste (see Tip, page 47).

17 **Sugar shaper discs** A selection of shapes to provide different effects.

18 **Small circle cutters** For cutting circle shapes for eyes.

19 **Plunger cutters** Flower plunger cutters used for adding detail.

20 **Measuring spoons** For accurate amounts of ingredients.

21 **Plastic circle cutters** Flat cutters used for scales on the Bubbles the Fish cake.

22 **Pastry cutter** For cutting large circles of cake e.g. for tractor wheels.

23 **Calyx cutter** For star decoration.

24 **Flower cutter** To cut large flowers e.g. for the Cosy Coupé cake.

25 **Scissors** For cutting templates from either paper, card or flexible plastic.

26 **Craft knife** For delicate cutting tasks e.g. the detail on the Fighter Jet cake.

27 **Cutting wheel (PME)** Used instead of a knife to avoid dragging the paste and excellent for texturing fur.

28 **Cocktail stick (toothpick)** Used for adding tiny patterns and details.

29 **Dresden tool** To create markings e.g. on the Wilbur Walrus cake.

30 **Ball tool** Makes even indentations, such as eyes prior to adding details.

31 **Textured rolling pin (HP)** Used to create fabric effect e.g. on Ballet Star.

32 **Zigzag cutter (FMM)** For zigzag pattern e.g. on Skippy Birthday cake.

33 **Quilting embosser (PC)** For adding quilted detail, such as to the underskirt layer of Princess Penny's dress.

Recipes

The main elements of all the cakes, including the madeira cake itself, can all be bought ready made if you wish. However, it is very easy (and often a lot cheaper) to make the main ingredients yourself. Here are my recipes:

SUGARPASTE (rolled fondant) Makes 625g (1lb 6oz)

Ready-made sugarpaste can be obtained from supermarkets and cake decorating suppliers. It is available in white as well as a whole multitude of colours. White paste allows you to make your own colours, whilst ready-coloured paste, particularly in red and black, is also useful. Alternatively, you can make your own sugarpaste using the recipe below:

450g (1lb/4 cups) sifted icing (confectioner's) sugar
1 egg white
30ml (2 tablespoons) liquid glucose
White vegetable fat (shortening) if required

1 Place the sugar in a mixing bowl. Make a well in the centre and add the egg white and glucose.
2 Mix it together with a spoon, and then knead it with your hands until all the sugar is mixed in. If the paste is a little dry, add some white vegetable fat and knead again.
3 The paste can be used straight away or stored in a plastic bag until required.

PASTILLAGE Makes 350g (12oz)

This is an extremely useful paste because, unlike modelling paste, it sets extremely hard and is not affected by moisture in the way that other pastes are. The down side to this, however, is that the paste tends to crust very quickly and, when it dries, it becomes brittle. You can buy it in a powdered form to which you add water but it is very easy to make it yourself. This is the recipe I use:

1 egg white
275g (10oz/2½ cups) sifted icing (confectioner's) sugar
10ml (2 teaspoons) gum tragacanth

1 Put the egg white into a large bowl, gradually adding and mixing in enough icing sugar to make a very stiff royal icing. Mix in the gum tragacanth – a natural gum. Turn the paste out onto your work surface and knead it.
2 If you require some softer pastillage to make items with a sugar shaper, place some to one side and then incorporate the remaining icing sugar into the rest to give a stiff paste. Store the pastillage in a polythene bag and place it in an airtight container in a refrigerator.

MODELLING PASTE

This versatile paste keeps its shape well, dries harder than sugarpaste and is used throughout the book for adding detail to covered cakes. Although there are commercial pastes readily available, it is very easy to make your own. This is the method I use:

5ml (1 teaspoon) gum tragacanth
225g (8oz) sugarpaste (rolled fondant)

Carefully knead the gum tragacanth into the sugarpaste. Wrap the paste in a plastic bag and allow the gum to work before using it. You will begin to feel a difference in the paste after an hour or so, but it is best to leave it overnight.

Note: If you have added a lot of colour to your paste and it is consequently very soft, an extra pinch or two of gum will be necessary. The modelling paste should be firm but pliable with a slightly elastic texture. If, on the other hand, once warmed your paste is still too hard, add a touch of white vegetable fat and a little boiled water and knead until it is softened.

Make a well in the centre of a ball of sugarpaste. Add the gum tragacanth and carefully knead it in.

SUGAR GLUE

Sugar glue is now available commercially. However, it is very quick and easy (and a lot cheaper) to make your own. There are many ways to do this but I make sugar glue as follows:

White modelling paste
Boiled water

Break up pieces of white modelling paste into an eggcup and cover with boiling water. Allow the water to dissolve the paste, stirring it to quicken the process. This produces a thick, strong glue, which can, if required, be thinned easily by adding some more boiled water. If really strong glue is required, use pastillage as the base rather than modelling paste.

Cover the broken pieces of modelling paste with boiled water.

LINING TINS

Measure the circumference of your tin and cut a greaseproof (wax) or baking paper strip slightly longer than this measurement to allow for an overlap. Make the strip 5cm (2in) deeper than the height of the tin. Fold up 2.5cm (1in) along the bottom of the strip. For a round tin, cut this fold with diagonal cuts, for a square or rectangular tin, crease the strip at intervals equal to the length of the inside edges of the tin and then cut the folded section into mitres. Grease the tin and place the strip around the sides with the cut edge on the base. Cut a piece of greaseproof or baking paper to fit the base. For bowls and ball tins, place a small circle of greaseproof paper in the base.

For a multisize pan, fit the cut strip of paper around the inside of the section you have chosen to use.

For a round tin, you need to cut a strip of paper for the sides of the tin and a circle of paper for the base.

BUTTERCREAM

Buttercream is used to sandwich cakes together as well as to coat them before covering with sugarpaste. Spreading buttercream over the sponge will fill any holes and give you a smooth surface on which to apply the sugarpaste.

115g (4oz/½ cup) butter
350g (12oz/3 cups) icing (confectioner's) sugar
15-30ml (1-2 tablespoons) milk or water
A few drops of vanilla extract (optional)

Place the butter in a bowl and beat until light and fluffy. Sift the icing sugar into the bowl and beat until the mixture changes colour. Add just enough milk or water to give a firm but spreadable consistency. Add the vanilla extract, then store in an airtight container until required.

Carefully sift the icing sugar into the beaten butter using a sieve. Gently shake the sieve or tap it with your hand to work the sugar through.

Use a plastic or wooden spatula to beat the sugar into the butter. Continue beating the mixture until all the sugar is incorporated.

MADEIRA CAKE

This cake is ideal for novelty cakes. It will keep for up to two weeks – I allow one week to decorate and one week to eat! See the chart below for quantities.

1 Pre-heat oven to 160ºC (325ºF or Gas Mark 3).
2 Grease and line the cake tin or bowl.
3 Cream the butter and sugar in a large bowl until light and fluffy.
4 Sift the flours together in a separate bowl. Beat the eggs into the creamed mixture, one at a time – follow each with a spoonful of flour.
5 Sift the remaining flour and any flavouring into the mixture and fold in carefully with a large metal spoon.
6 Transfer the mixture to the lined tin and bake. Baking times will depend on your oven, the tin and the depth of the cake. Check the cake after 1–1¼ hours. When the cake is baked, it will be well risen, firm to the touch and a skewer inserted into the centre will come out clean. Allow to cool and, leaving the paper on, wrap in foil or place in an airtight container for at least 12 hours.

FLAVOURINGS

Traditionally madeira is flavoured with lemon but I have listed other flavours you may wish to try. These are for a 6 egg cake (increase or decrease the amounts as needed):

Lemon grated rind of two lemons
Cherry 350g (12oz) glacé cherries, halved
Fruit 350g (12oz) sultanas, currants, raisins or dates
Coconut 115g (4oz) desiccated coconut
Nut Replace 250g (9oz/2¼ cups) flour with ground almonds or hazelnuts.

BAKING CHART - MADEIRA CAKE QUANTITIES

Cakes	Bake ware	Eggs (large)	Butter	Caster sugar (superfine)	Self raising flour	Plain flour (all purpose)	Baking times @ 160°C (325°F/Gas Mark 3)
Roger Rabbit p.14	25.5cm (10in) square tin	10	550g (1lb 4oz/2½ cups)	550 g (1lb 4oz/2½ cups)	550g (1lb 4oz/5 cups)	275g (10oz/2½ cups)	1½–1¾ hours
Princess Penny p.18	2 x 15cm (6in) round tins	6	350g (12oz/1½ cups)	350g (12oz/1½ cups)	350g (12oz/3 cups)	175g (6oz/1½ cups)	1¼–1½ hours
Space Monster p.22	2 x 15cm (6in) round tins and 7.5cm (3in) round food can	7	400g (14oz/1¾ cups)	400g (14oz/1¾ cups)	400g (14oz/3½ cups)	200g (7oz/1¾ cups)	1½ hours
Harvest Tractor p.26	25.5cm (10in) round tin and 12.5cm (5in) square tin	8	450g (1lb/2 cups)	450g (1lb/2 cups)	450g (1lb/4 cups)	225g (8oz/2 cups)	1¼ hours
Tristan's Shark p.30	10cm x 30cm (4in x 12in) rectangular tin (multisized cake pan)	5	275g (10oz/1¼ cups)	275g (10oz/1¼ cups)	275g (10oz/2½ cups)	150g/ (5oz/¾ cup)	1¼–1½ hours
Suzie Strawberry p.34	20cm (8in) heart tin	5	275g (10oz/1¼ cups)	275g (10oz/1¼ cups)	275g (10oz/2½ cups)	150g/ (5oz/¾ cup)	1¼–1½ hours
Ballet star p.37	25.5cm (10in) round tin	7	400g (14oz/1¾ cups)	400g (14oz/1¾ cups)	400g (14oz/3½ cups)	200g (7oz/1¾ cups)	1½ hours
Carl Caterpillar p.40	20cm (8in) square tin	7	400g (14oz/1¾ cups)	400g (14oz/1¾ cups)	400g (14oz/3½ cups)	200g (7oz/1¾ cups)	1½ hours
Cosy Coupé p.44	30.5cm x 20cm (12in x 8in) rectangular tin (multisized cake pan)	10	550g (1lb 4oz/2½ cups)	550g (1lb 4oz/2½ cups)	550g (1lb 4oz/5 cups)	275g (10oz/2½ cups)	1½–1¾ hours
Wilbur Walrus p.48	23cm (9in) square tin	8	450g (1lb/2 cups)	450g (1lb/2 cups)	450g (1lb/4 cups)	225g (8oz/2 cups)	1¾ hours
Party Dog p.52	20cm (8in) square tin	6	350g (12oz/1½ cups)	350g (12oz/1½ cups)	350g (12oz/3 cups)	175g (6oz/1½ cups)	1¼–1½ hours
Skippy Birthday p.56	23cm x 13cm (9in x 5in) (multisized) tin and 8cm (3⅛in) round food can	6	350g (12oz/1½ cups)	350g (12oz/1½ cups)	350g (12oz/3 cups)	175g (6oz/1½ cups)	1¼–1½ hours
Bee Happy p.60	15cm (6in) ball tin	6	350g (12oz/1½ cups)	350g (12oz/1½ cups)	350g (12oz/3 cups)	175g (6oz/1½ cups)	1¼–1½ hours
Clever Cat p.64	2 x 15cm (6in) round tins and 1 x 10cm (4in) round tin	8	450g (1lb/2 cups)	450g (1lb/2 cups)	450g (1lb/4 cups)	225g (8oz/2 cups)	1½ hours
Space Shuttle p.68	15cm (6in) ball tin	6	350g (12oz/1½ cups)	350g (12oz/1½ cups)	350g (12oz/3 cups)	175g (6oz/1½ cups)	1¼–1½ hours
Lucky Ladybird p.72	1 litre (2 pint/5 cup) pudding basin and 8cm (3⅛ in) round food can	5	275g (10oz/1¼ cups)	275g (10oz/1¼ cups)	275g (10oz/2½ cups)	150g/ (5oz/1¼ cups)	1¼–1½ hours
Shape Sorter p.76	2 x 15cm (6in) square tin	8	450g (1lb/2 cups)	450g (1lb/2 cups)	450g (1lb/4 cups)	225g (8oz/2 cups)	1½ hours
Bubbles the Fish p.80	3 litre/6 pint/15 cup ovenproof bowl	6	350g (12oz/1½ cups)	350g (12oz/1½ cups)	350g (12oz/3 cups)	175g (6oz/1½ cups)	1¼–1½ hours
Fighter Jet p.84	20cm (8in) round tin	6	350g (12oz/1½ cups)	350g (12oz/1½ cups)	350g (12oz/3 cups)	175g (6oz/1½ cups)	1¼–1½ hours
Smiley Face p.88	3 litre/6 pint/15 cup ovenproof bowl	6	350g (12oz/1½ cups)	350g (12oz/1½ cups)	350g (12oz/3 cups)	175g (6oz/1½ cups)	1¼–1½ hours

Covering Cakes and Boards

To be confident of creating an even covering of sugarpaste (rolled fondant), you need to master a few simple techniques.

🎈 COVERING CAKES

Knead the sugarpaste until it is warm and pliable. Roll it on a surface lightly sprinkled with icing (confectioner's) sugar, to a depth of 5mm (¼in). It is a good idea to use spacers when you roll it out so that you achieve an even thickness. Cover the cake in a thin layer of buttercream to help the sugarpaste stick to it. Then, lift the paste carefully over the top of the cake, supporting it with a rolling pin, and position the sugarpaste so that it covers the cake.

Smooth the surface of the cake to remove any lumps and bumps using a smoother for the flat areas and the palm of your hand for the curved areas. Always make sure that your hands are clean and dry (with no traces of icing sugar) before smoothing. Trim away the excess paste with a knife – it often helps to mark a cutting line with a smoother, by pressing the smoother down around the edge of the cake into the excess paste before trimming.

Should you find that you have unwanted air bubbles under the sugarpaste, insert a clean dressmaker's pin at an angle and gently press the air out.

Roll the sugarpaste out between spacers to achieve an even thickness.

Use a rolling pin to support the sugarpaste as you lift it over the buttercreamed cake.

Use a smoother to even out the surface and to mark cutting lines for the excess.

Use a sharp knife to cut away the excess sugarpaste from around the base of the cake.

🎈 BOARDS

Roll out the sugarpaste to a depth of 4mm (⅛in), ideally using spacers. Moisten the board with water or sugar glue. Lift up the paste and drape it over the board. Circle a smoother over the paste to achieve a smooth flat finish to the board. Cut the paste flush with the sides of the board, taking care to keep the edge vertical. The covered board should then be left to dry thoroughly.

🎈 STORING CAKES

Store your decorated cake in a cardboard cake box and keep it in a warm, dry place – never in a refrigerator.

TIP

★ *Spacers allow you to achieve an even thickness of paste. You can make 4mm (⅛in) and 5mm (¼in) spacers from strips of wood, available from DIY stores.*

Colour Mixing

It is helpful to be aware of the basics of colour theory. The visible colour spectrum consists of three primary colours from which all colours are made. Any colour can be created through a combination of these primary colours, together with black and white.

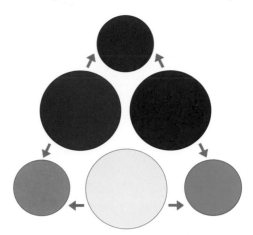

Use paste food colours in each of the three primary colours – red, blue and yellow – to practise mixing colours. Create secondary colours – purple, green and orange – by mixing two primaries in equal amounts.

Whether you are colouring paste or painting, have a go at mixing colours together so that you get a feel for how you can achieve different tones, shades and hues. You may have to use a little trial and error before you get the exact shade you require, so practise first.

COLOURING PASTE

It is always better to colour your paste in natural light as artificial light greatly alters certain colours. Depending on the amount of paste you wish to colour and the depth of colour required, place either a little paste food colour (not liquid colour) on the end of a cocktail stick (toothpick) or a larger amount on the end of a palette knife. Add the colour to the paste and knead in thoroughly, adding more until the desired result is achieved.

Be careful with pale colours because only a little colour will be needed. Deep colours, on the other hand, require a lot of colour and the paste will become quite sticky. In order to overcome this, add a pinch of gum tragacanth and leave it for an hour or two to make the paste firmer and easier to handle. Remember that the coloured paste will appear slightly darker when it is dry.

Knead the colour into the paste little by little until you get the desired shade.

PAINTING

Many fabulous effects can be achieved by painting over dried sugarpaste. Painting also helps to brighten the overall appearance of a cake because even vividly coloured paste will dry with a dull finish. Paste food colours behave in much the same way as ordinary water based paints in that you can mix them to produce all sorts of tones and hues.

To paint sugarpaste (rolled fondant), dilute some paste food colour in a clear spirit, such as gin or vodka, and, using either a paintbrush, damp natural sponge or stippling brush, carefully apply the colour to the dry sugarpaste. For deep colours, just add a little clear spirit to some paste food colour and for light colours add a touch of colour to some clear spirit. (For details of flood painting see Smiley Face, pages 88–90).

For a variety of effects, you can use a paintbrush to apply diluted colours.

Roger Rabbit

There is nothing more alluring than a fluffy little rabbit twitching his nose or bobbing his tail as he scampers around. Roger Rabbit is no exception! Children will love his brown and white fur and little pink nose. Watch out though, he's after those cabbage leaves!

CAKE AND DECORATION

10 egg 25.5cm (10in) square madeira cake (see page 11)

33cm (13in) round cake board

1.84kg (4lb 1oz) sugarpaste (rolled fondant)

Straw-yellow, brown, black and green paste food colours

25g (1oz) pastillage

Half quantity of buttercream

White vegetable fat (shortening)

Sugar glue

Fresh cabbage leaves

Clear spirit, such as gin or vodka

Pink dusting powder

Confectioner's glaze

110cm (40in) gold ribbon

EQUIPMENT

Carving knife

Rabbit templates (see page 91)

Foam pad or kitchen paper

Waxed paper

Non-stick work board

Cutting wheel/dresden tool/ craft knife

Large-headed paintbrush

Circle cutter: 1cm (½in)

STAGE ONE

1 **Colouring the pastes** Colour all but 200g (7oz) of the white sugarpaste (rolled fondant) as follows: 600g (1lb 5oz) brown, 1kg (2lb 3oz) straw-yellow (for the board), 25g (1oz) green, 15g (½oz) black. Colour the pastillage a pale brown.

2 **Covering the board** Roll out the straw-coloured sugarpaste and cover the board, trimming the sugarpaste flush with the edge. Take a large carving knife and randomly cut into the soft sugarpaste to create the straw effect (see picture **a**). Place to one side to dry.

3 **Making the leaves** Roll out the green sugarpaste and cut out rough leaf shapes. Place one of the pieces between two dry, fresh cabbage leaves and gently press to make the veins (see picture **b**). Curl the edges to give movement to the leaf and allow to dry. Repeat to make more cabbage leaves.

4 **Making the ears** Smear your work board with white vegetable fat (shortening) and thinly roll out the pastillage. Using the ear template, cut out two ear shapes. Leave the paste on the board for a minute or two, then transfer to a foam pad or kitchen paper for a further minute. Finally, pinch the base of the ear together, support in position and leave to dry.

a *Make cuts over the surface of the yellow sugarpaste to resemble straw.*

b *Gently press the sugarpaste leaf shape between two fresh cabbage leaves.*

STAGE TWO

5 **Preparing the cake** Level the cake and remove the crust from the base. Cut in half vertically. Spread a thin layer of buttercream over the top of one half of the cake and stack the other half on top. Freeze until firm.

STAGE THREE

6 **Carving the cake** Make the rabbit templates and place the top template in position on top of the cake. With a large knife, cut vertically down through the cakes around the template, removing small sections at a time. Place the profile template on one long side of the cake and cut around it to create the basic rabbit shape (see picture). Mark the position of the hind legs and the head by cutting into the cake along the lines on the template. Remove the template, and curve and shape all the cut edges paying particular attention to the shape of the head, which is wider at its base.

7 **Covering the cake** Place the cake on waxed paper and cover the back section (as indicated on the template) with a thin layer of buttercream (see picture ⓓ). Cover this section with brown sugarpaste, trim into shape and smooth the cut edge flat over the rabbit's body. Next, take a cutting wheel, dresden tool or craft knife and repeatedly cut short lines into the paste to create textured fur (the quickest way to create this effect is with a cutting wheel). Cover the section between the brown paste and the rabbit's neck with buttercream. Roll out the white sugarpaste and cut a 5cm (2in) wide strip. Make one long edge slightly thinner with a rolling pin then, whilst the paste is still on the work surface, cut into the thinned paste with the cutting wheel, dresden tool or craft knife to create an irregular edge. Place this strip in position, overlapping the textured edge with the body of the rabbit. Trim to fit, then texture the paste.

8 **Covering the head** Applying a thin layer of buttercream only to the section you are about to work on, cover the head in stages. First, cover the lower head area with a 3cm (1¼in) wide strip of white sugarpaste. Trim to size and add texture (the join where this paste meets the neck will disappear with texturing). Next, take the brown sugarpaste and cut out a shape

ⓒ *Using the templates, carve away the frozen cake to form the basic rabbit shape.*

ⓓ *Cover the rabbit's back with a thin layer of buttercream before adding the sugarpaste.*

ⓔ *Cut a piece of sugarpaste for each side of the face and texture the edge.*

16

to cover one side of the face. Thin the edge that will meet the body and texture this edge on your work surface as before (see picture (e)). Place on the cake and texture all but the eye area. Repeat for the other side of the head. Cut and position a white sugarpaste triangle on the front of the head then texture. Texturing the straight cut edges gives an irregular edge (see picture (f)).

 Adding the features For the nose take a 2cm (¾in) ball of white sugarpaste, pinch half of it into a point to make the nose shape and flatten the other half. Glue the nose in position and blend the flattened paste into the white fur by texturing it. Cut a 'Y' into the paste directly under the nose, then make small holes either side for whiskers (see picture (g)). Insert the pastillage ears and secure in place.

 Painting the board Dilute straw-yellow paste colour in clear spirit and, using a large-headed paintbrush, apply the colour to the board. The colour will sink into the cut surface, highlighting the texture. Allow to dry.

STAGE FOUR

11 **Adding rabbit details** Transfer the rabbit to the board. Roll out and texture four strips of brown sugarpaste and attach to either side of each ear (see picture (h)). Using the ear template, cut two pieces of paste for the backs of the ears, texture and glue in place. Model a teardrop of white sugarpaste for the tail, attach and texture. Make the hind feet in the same way.

12 **Making the eyes** Roll a 1.5cm (⅝in) ball of green paste. Cut in half and attach to the face. Cut pupils from black paste using the circle cutter, add light spots and attach. Roll thin sausages of brown paste and place around each eye. Blend this paste into the rabbit's fur with a cutting wheel.

13 **Adding the final touches** Paint the rabbit to highlight his fur by using brown paste colour diluted in clear spirit. Attach the leaves to the board and paint with a colour wash. Brush a little pink dust over the nose and add confectioner's glaze to the eye. Attach the ribbon around the board.

(f) *Once the rabbit is completely covered, texture the straight edges to blend in.*

(g) *Make a flattened ball of white sugarpaste for the nose and texture it into the white fur.*

(h) *Add brown fur details to the front and back of the pastillage ear shapes.*

17

Princess Penny

Lots of little girls like nothing better than to dress up in sparkling splendour, imagining a fairytale land of princesses and make believe. This cake incorporates a doll, which could double as a birthday gift to be kept and treasured for future adventures.

CAKE AND DECORATION

6 egg madeira baked in
2 x 15cm (6in) round tins
(see page 11)

28cm (11in) round cake board

1.6kg (3lb 8oz) white sugarpaste
(rolled fondant)

Lilac, purple and ruby paste
food colours

Half quantity of buttercream

A 30cm (12in) doll

Gum tragacanth

White vegetable fat (shortening)

Lilac lustre dust

Sugar glue

Silver dragées

1m (39in) silver ribbon or braid

EQUIPMENT

Carving knives, including one
with a long, thin blade

Waxed paper

Smoother

Non-stick work board

Sugar shaper (optional)

Mini quilting embosser (PC)

Paintbrush

Scissors

Cutting wheel/craft knife

Plunger flower cutters

STAGE ONE

1 **Covering the board** Colour 500g (1lb 2oz) sugarpaste (rolled fondant) lilac. Roll out the paste and cover the board, trimming the sugarpaste flush with the edge. Leave to dry. Place the trimmings to one side.

STAGE TWO

2 **Preparing the cake for freezing** Level the cakes and remove the crusts from their bases. Spread a thin layer of buttercream over the top of one of the cakes and stack the other on top. With a long, thin bladed knife, cut into the very centre of the top cake and push vertically down through the cakes to the base. With the knife in this position, cut out and remove a 4.5cm (1¾in) wide cylinder to make space for the doll's legs. Wrap the doll's legs in cling film (or other food-safe plastic) and place her in position inside the cake to ensure she fits. Adjust the cake, if necessary, so that the doll stands with her waist around 3cm (1¼in) proud of the cake. Remove the doll. Freeze the cake until firm.

STAGE THREE

3 **Shaping the cake** Take a large knife and start to shape the cake (see cutting guide). It is best to remove a little at a time until you are happy with the shape (see picture **a**). Do not worry about getting it completely smooth as much of the cake will be covered in layers of 'fabric'.

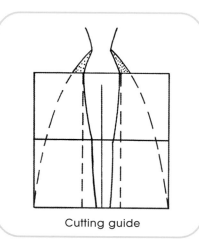

Cutting guide

a *Gently shape the cake 'skirt' using a carving knife, removing a little at a time.*

Short cuts

⏱ Use a large tiffin tin to bake the cake – it will save carving time.

⏱ You can buy 'legless' dolls from cake-decorating shops but be aware that your cake's recipient may be disappointed if the doll has no legs!

⏱ Omit the quilting process or the quilted layer.

⏱ Omit the lustre dusts.

⏱ Simplify the decorative details.

⏱ Omit the trim from the edges of the skirt.

TIPS

★ If your doll is a lot smaller than the suggested size, you may find that a cake cooked in a pudding bowl or small tiffin tin would make a more appropriate skirt.

★ If you do not have a sugar shaper, you can easily cut strips by hand – a sugar shaper just saves you time.

4 **Covering the cake** Place the cake on waxed paper. Spread a thin layer of buttercream over the outside of the cake to help stick the sugarpaste. Roll out the white sugarpaste and cover the cake, gently easing in the fullness. Trim the paste around the base and remove it from above the hole at the top of the cake. Reinsert the wrapped doll in position and, using another piece of white sugarpaste, build up her skirt so it reaches her waist. Ease into shape using a smoother and blend the join with your fingers. Leave to dry.

5 **Mixing the modelling pastes** To create modelling pastes, add 2.5ml (½ teaspoon) gum tragacanth to 100g (3½ oz) lilac sugarpaste trimmings. Colour another 50g (2oz) of the trimmings a deep purple and add 1.25ml (¼ teaspoon) gum. Then colour 300g (11oz) sugarpaste trimmings a rich purple using purple and a touch of ruby – knead in 7.5ml (1½ teaspoons) gum. Allow the gum to take effect, preferably overnight.

STAGE FOUR

6 **Trimming the hem** Remove the cake from the waxed paper and transfer it to the centre of the covered board. Soften some deep purple modelling paste by adding white vegetable fat (shortening) and boiled water, and knead until malleable. Place the paste in a sugar shaper with the medium-sized ribbon disc. Squeeze out a length of paste and stick it to the hem of the skirt. Replace the paste and disc in the shaper with some softened lilac paste and the small ribbon disc. Squeeze out another length and position this on top of the first.

7 **Adding the quilted skirt** Knead the lilac modelling paste until warm, adding a little white vegetable fat if it feels stiff. Smear your work board with white vegetable fat and thinly roll out the paste into a strip. Take a mini quilting embosser and, carefully but firmly, press it into the paste. Remove the embosser, line up the pattern and press into the paste twice more to create a strip of textured paste. Using a paintbrush, dust the surface of the paste with the lilac lustre dust to give a sheen (see picture ⓑ). Place glue around the waist of the doll and stick the strip in position down the skirt to represent one layer of her dress. Trim the lower edge of the strip with scissors. Repeat for the other side.

ⓑ *Use an embosser to create the quilted pattern, then dust with lilac lustre dust.*

ⓒ *Glue the textured paste in place to make the bodice and the quilted skirt layer.*

ⓓ *To make the waist drape, gather the rolled paste at each end and form a loop.*

8 **Making the bodice** Texture another strip of lilac modelling paste and apply lilac lustre dust in the same way as before. Apply glue to the doll's waist and down her front and underarm seams. Place a section of textured paste horizontally over her front so it overlaps the quilted skirt layer. With a cutting wheel or craft knife, cut down the centre front and side seams so that the paste forms half of the bodice front. Repeat for the second half of the bodice (see picture) and then make the back in the same way. Thinly roll out some rich purple modelling paste and cut into a 9cm x 6cm (3½in x 2½ in) rectangle. Gather the shorter sides and position the gathered ends on each shoulder so the paste drapes slightly over the front of her bodice. Trim and repeat for the back.

9 **Making the overskirt** Thinly roll out the rich purple modelling paste into a large rectangle approximately 40cm x 25cm (16in x 10in). On one long side, cut two corners into a gradual curve and pleat the other long side. Paint a line of glue around the princess's waist and attach the pleated paste. Trim at the waist as necessary.

10 **Making the drapes** Thinly roll out some of the rich purple paste and cut into a rectangle. Gather both short sides and bring together to form a loop (see picture) and attach to the waist. For the flower decoration, cut flowers from thinly rolled paste using a plunger cutter (see picture e). Stick a silver dragée in the centre of each flower. (Note: dragées can tarnish quickly in a slightly moist atmosphere so make sure you store your finished cake in a dry place).

11 **Adding the trim (optional)** Soften some dark purple modelling paste by adding a little white vegetable fat and cooled boiled water and place in a sugar shaper together with the small round disc. Squeeze out a length around the cut edge of the overskirt. Repeat for the quilted skirt layer using the lilac paste (see picture f). Finally, attach a ribbon around the board using non-toxic glue, holding it in place with dressmaking pins. Remove the pins once the ribbon is fixed (see picture g).

e Use a plunger cutter for the flowers. Attach them directly from the cutter to the dress.

f Using a sugar shaper, gently squeeze out and apply trim to the edges of the princess's skirt.

g Hold the ribbon or braid in place with dressmaking pins while the glue dries.

Space Monster

Monsters need not necessarily be scary and bad. Look who's just landed! This fun space alien is certainly a friendly beast and would make a welcome addition to any young earthling's birthday table. You can let your imagination run wild with the monster's decoration.

CAKE AND DECORATION

7 egg madeira cake baked in 2 x 15cm (6in) round tins and a 7.5cm (3in) food can (see page 11)

30.5cm (12in) round cake board

Sugarpaste (rolled fondant):
600g (1lb 5oz) red,
1.1kg (2lb 7oz) light green,
75g (3oz) yellow,
25g (1oz) white

Icing (confectioner's) sugar

Green, yellow and black paste food colours

25g (1oz) pastillage

Half quantity of buttercream

Gum tragacanth

Sugar glue

1m (39in) red ribbon

EQUIPMENT

Knife

Ball tool

Smoother

Monster templates (see page 91)

Dresden tool

Indenting tool/dowel

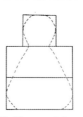

Cutting guide

STAGE ONE

1 **Covering the board** Roll out the red sugarpaste (rolled fondant), using icing (confectioner's) sugar to prevent it sticking. Cover the board, trimming the sugarpaste flush with the edge. Press a ball tool into the soft paste to make the craters (see picture). Make circular motions with the tool to enlarge the holes, then create ripples by pressing and dragging the tool through the paste. Circle a finger over the indented rings to soften their edges.

2 **Making the antennae** Colour the pastillage yellow, then roll it into a sausage and cut two 7cm (2¾in) lengths. Curve each piece slightly and leave to dry.

STAGE TWO

3 **Preparing the cake for freezing** Level the cakes and remove the crusts from their bases. Spread buttercream over the top of the two larger cakes. Stack the cakes with the small cake on top. Freeze until firm.

STAGE THREE

4 **Carving the cake** First, round all the edges of the small cake to make the head. Then, carve the main body cakes by cutting away all the edges to form the monster's tummy (see picture and cutting guide).

 Use a ball tool to make indentations around the board, representing craters.

 Carve the cake by rounding off all the edges on the head and body sections.

Short cuts

⏱ Omit the freezing stage.

⏱ Use sugar cigarette sweets rather than pastillage for the antennae.

⏱ Use ready-coloured sugarpaste.

⏱ Omit the yellow dot decoration from the monster's body.

⏱ Simplify the shape of the arms and feet.

5 **Covering the head cake** Cover the head section with a thin layer of buttercream to stick the sugarpaste. Roll out some light green sugarpaste and cover the head, pulling up the excess paste at the back of the head to form a pleat – cut this away (see picture ⓒ). Smooth the join closed and trim away the excess paste at the neck.

6 **Covering the body** Cover the body with a thin layer of buttercream. Roll out the remaining light green sugarpaste and cut it into a 16cm (6½in) wide strip. Wrap this strip around the body so the join is at the back. Cut off the excess paste and smooth the join closed. Ease the paste under the body at the base and trim to fit if necessary. Place the trimmings to one side. Blend the neck join away with your fingers. It should disappear completely, but if it does not, do not worry – a strategically placed yellow patch should hide it!

7 **Making the patches** Roll pieces of the yellow sugarpaste into balls, flatten slightly then press them onto the green sugarpaste, using a smoother or the base of your hand (see picture ⓓ). I have flattened my patches completely so the monster's body is smooth but you could leave them standing proud. To create the monster's bellybutton, gently press a ball tool into the centre of his tummy.

8 **Mixing colours** Take 200g (7oz) of the light green sugarpaste trimmings and add some darker green paste colour (this paste will be used for the feet and arms). Take a further 25g (1oz) of the light green paste and add a generous pinch of gum tragacanth to make modelling paste for the ears. Add another generous pinch of gum to the white sugarpaste and 1.25ml (¼ teaspoon) gum to 50g (2oz) of the red sugarpaste. Allow the gum to take effect.

STAGE FOUR

9 **Making the feet** Make a foot template from paper or card. Thickly roll out some of the darker green sugarpaste and cut out the feet using the template and a knife. Smooth the cut edges with your finger (see picture ⓔ) and attach the feet to the bottom of the cake.

ⓒ *Cover the head section with light green sugarpaste and cut the excess away.*

ⓓ *Use a smoother to create an even finish on the yellow patches.*

ⓔ *Cut two feet from the light green sugarpaste and smooth all cut edges with your fingers.*

 10 **Making the arms** Roll two 10cm (4in) long sausages of the darker green paste to form the monster's arms. Thin them at one end to form wrists by rolling the sausage between your fingers. Then, make two cuts in each 'hand' to form fingers. Flatten each finger and smooth all the cut edges (see picture ⓕ). Cut the upper arms at an angle so that they fit neatly onto the body. Glue both arms in position.

 11 **Making the nose** For the monster's nose, roll red sugarpaste to form a 3.5cm (1⅜in) wide ball. Slice away a section so that it will easily attach to the face and glue in position with sugar glue. Indent the nostrils with a suitable tool.

 12 **Making the eyes** For the eyes, roll a 3.5cm (1⅜in) ball of white paste and cut in half (this ensures that both eyes are the same size). Roll each half into a ball and attach them to the face. Colour the remaining green modelling paste black and use this to make small flattened balls for pupils.

13 **Making the mouth** For the monster's mouth, roll a thin sausage of the remaining black modelling paste and glue into a smile. Add teeth cut from the white paste.

14 **Making the ears** Make a template from paper or card and cut two ears from the green modelling paste. Indent the markings with a dresden tool (see picture ⓖ) and curve the ears slightly to add movement. Glue both ears in position.

15 **Attaching the antennae** Roll four small balls of red paste for the base and tips of the antennae. Carefully indent holes in these using a dowel and glue them onto the dried yellow pastillage (see picture ⓗ). Place the antennae in position on the monster's head by carefully pushing the pastillage into the cake until they are secure. Finally, attach a ribbon around the board with non-toxic glue.

ⓕ *Flatten each of the fingers and smooth all the cut edges.*

ⓖ *Cut ears from the modelling paste. Add markings and gently curve the edges.*

ⓗ *Make two red sugarpaste balls and indent them to fit on the ends of the antennae.*

25

Harvest Tractor

The busy blue tractor has been chugging along in the field since the early hours with nothing but the sound of the birds calling overhead to accompany it. The farmer has certainly got his work cut out – this field of corn is ready and waiting to be harvested.

CAKE AND DECORATION

8 egg madeira split between a 25.5cm (10in) round tin and a 12.5cm (5in) square tin (see page 11)

25.5cm (10in) thin round cake board

Sugarpaste (rolled fondant):
250g (9oz) black,
450g (1lb) blue,
1kg (2lb 3oz) white

Brown and golden brown paste food colours

One quantity of buttercream

Gum tragacanth

Sugar glue

50g (2oz) pastillage

White vegetable fat (shortening)

Clear spirit, such as gin or vodka

EQUIPMENT

Tractor templates (see page 94)

Strong card for the formers

Narrow spacers

Cocktail stick (toothpick)

Large carving knife

Small sharp knife

Non-stick work board

Circle cutters:
8cm (3 in) pastry cutter, 4.5cm (1¾ in), 5.5cm (2¼ in), 2cm (¾ in)

Waxed paper

Dresden tool

Stiff bristled brush

Paintbrush

STAGE ONE

 Mixing pastes Add 2.5ml (½ teaspoon) gum tragacanth to 100g (3½oz) of the white sugarpaste (rolled fondant) and 1.25ml (¼ teaspoon) gum tragacanth to 50g (2oz) of the blue sugarpaste to make modelling pastes.

2 Making the mudguards Make two formers from card using the template as a guide. Thinly roll out some of the pastillage and cut two 2.5cm x 10cm (1in x 4in) strips. Use spacers when rolling out the pastillage to keep a uniform thickness (see picture ⓐ). Position on the formers and allow to dry.

3 Making the exhaust pipe Colour the remaining pastillage brown. Roll a 3.5cm x 1.5cm (1⅜in x ⅝in) cylinder, followed by two 5mm (¼in) wide lengths. Bend one length and make a hole in the top with a cocktail stick (toothpick) (see picture ⓑ). Glue the pieces together and allow to dry.

STAGE TWO

4 Preparing the cake Level the 12.5cm (5in) square cake then cut out a 10cm x 7.5cm (4in x 3in) rectangle. Freeze it for a few hours to make it easier to carve the wheel arches. From the remaining cake, cut a 6.5cm x 5cm (2¾ in x 2in) rectangle, then cut it to a height of 5cm (2in) for the engine section. Place in an airtight container or plastic bag and put to one side.

ⓐ *To make the mudguards, model strips of white pastillage over card formers.*

ⓑ *Make the exhaust pipe from three lengths of brown pastillage glued together.*

STAGE THREE

5 **Carving the tractor** Make a cab template. Take the frozen cake and, using a small sharp knife, cut out the wheel arches around the template to a depth of 1.5cm (⅝in). For the windscreen and the rear window of the cab, use the template and cut away the appropriate sections. Level the round cake and cut horizontally across the cake at a height of 4cm (1½in) to create the field. Place in an airtight container or plastic bag and put to one side.

6 **Making the wheels** Cut the wheels from the cut-off section of the round cake using the 8cm (3in) and 4.5cm (1¾in) circle cutters or the templates. Cut each large wheel to a depth of 2cm (¾in) and the small wheels to a depth of 1.5cm (⅝in). Make a hollow in the centre of each wheel using your finger (see picture). Then, cut across the circles as shown on the templates.

7 **Covering the cab** Assemble the sections and place them onto waxed paper (see picture). Spread buttercream over the part you are about to cover. Roll out the black sugarpaste and cut it into a 4.5cm (1¾in) wide strip. Wrap this around the top of the cab to form the windows. Trim away the excess paste and smooth the join closed. Make a 6cm (2½in) wide blue strip and wrap it around the rear of the tractor from one wheel recess to another. Trim and smooth to fit. Using another 6cm (2½in) wide strip, cover the lower front of the cab. Cover the roof with blue sugarpaste, trimming the edges flush with the black paste of the windows.

8 **Adding the mudguards** Attach the mudguards by gently pushing them through the soft paste. Cover the sides and front of the engine with blue sugarpaste and position in front of the cab. Position the exhaust pipe. Model a 2.5cm x 1.5cm x 1.5cm (1in x ⅝in x ⅝in) box from blue sugarpaste and place it in front of the engine then mark grooves with a knife. Allow to dry.

9 **Covering the wheels** Spread a thin layer of buttercream over one of the wheels. Roll out some of the black sugarpaste and place over the buttercream. Make a pleat of the excess paste at the rear of the wheel

c Use circle cutters or the templates to make the wheels. Indent the centres with your finger.

d Carve the cake into separate sections for the cab, engine and wheel arches.

e Cover the round cake with golden brown sugarpaste over a layer of buttercream.

and cut it away. Trim the paste flush with the base of the wheel, smooth and ease the paste into the recess. Using a dresden tool, make a herringbone pattern around the tyres for the tread. Fill the recesses with white modelling paste cut to size with a circle cutter. Decorate as desired then allow to dry.

STAGE FOUR

 Creating the field Colour the remaining white sugarpaste golden brown. Place the round cake on the 25.5cm (10in) board. Cover the cake with buttercream. Place the board on top of a smaller board or plate to lift it up. Cover the cake and trim the paste flush with the underside of the board (see picture). Press a brush into the paste to texture the corn (see picture). Drag a dresden tool up the sides of the cake for the corn stalks (see picture).

 Positioning the tractor Secure the sections of the tractor in position. Using a dresden tool to texture the paste, disguise the joins between the tractor and the field. Texture the flat corn around the tyres with sweeping strokes.

 Adding detail Add a trace of white vegetable fat (shortening) to the blue modelling paste and roll it out. Cut 4mm (³⁄₁₆in) wide strips for the windows and cover the join between the cab and engine. Cut a 6mm (¼in) wide strip and wrap it around the roof. Cut a 1cm (½in) wide strip and wrap it around the top of the engine. Add a small black strip. Roll out some white modelling paste and cut a rectangle for the grill, mark vertical lines and position.

 Finishing the tractor Thickly roll the remaining white paste and press it onto the roof. Remove the paste and trim it 2.5mm (⅛in) larger than the impression made by the roof. Smooth the edges and attach to the roof. Make the lights from black, white and golden brown paste (see picture ).

STAGE FIVE

 Colouring the field Dilute some golden brown paste colour in clear spirit and use a paintbrush to apply a colour wash to the field. This will intensify the colour and highlight the texturing (see above). Allow it to dry.

f Use a brush to texture the surface of the sugarpaste to resemble the tops of corn.

g Drag the dresden tool vertically through the paste around the sides of the cake.

h Use black, white and golden brown pieces of paste to make the lights.

Tristan's Shark

Sharks have a bad reputation but most sharks are not at all dangerous and attacks on people are very rare. Tristan's tiger shark is especially friendly and would make a wonderful centrepiece for anyone who is fascinated by these graceful creatures.

CAKE AND DECORATION

5 egg madeira cake baked in a 10cm x 30cm (4in x 12in) tin (a Multisize cake pan is ideal) (see page 11)

40cm x 30cm (16in x12in) cake board

2kg (4lb 6oz) white sugarpaste (rolled fondant)

Blue and black paste food colours

Half quantity of buttercream

50g (2oz) pastillage

Gum tragacanth

White dust food colour

White vegetable fat (shortening)

Sugar glue

Clear spirit, such as gin or vodka

Piping gel

1.5m (60in) blue or white ribbon

EQUIPMENT

Shark templates (see pages 92–93)

Non-stick work board

Small knife/cutting wheel (PME)

Kitchen paper/foam

Carving knife

Dresden tool

Waxed paper

Paintbrushes

STAGE ONE

1 **Covering the board** Take 1.3kg (2lb 14oz) of the sugarpaste (rolled fondant). Divide it up into several pieces and colour these in different shades of blue by using varying amounts of the blue colouring. Roughly knead the sugarpaste pieces together then roll into a long sausage shape. Cut the sausage in half lengthways to reveal the marbled pattern inside (see picture **a**). Place the two halves next to each other, cut-side up, and smooth over the join. Roll out the paste and use to cover the board.

2 **Colouring the paste** Colour all but 25g (1oz) of the remaining sugarpaste a light grey. Using the black paste colour, add a small amount of the blue to create a blue-grey. Take 100g (3½oz) of the blue-grey paste and knead in 5ml (1 teaspoon) gum tragacanth to make modelling paste.

3 **Making the fins** Make the templates. Roll out the pastillage, using a smear of white vegetable fat (shortening) to stop it sticking to your work board. Place a template on the paste and cut around it, ideally with a cutting wheel, as this does not drag the paste. Repeat the process for the other fins and tail, cutting two where indicated (see picture **b**). Transfer the fins to a porous surface such as foam or kitchen paper and allow to dry in a warm place – an airing cupboard, if you have one, is ideal for this.

a *Knead the different shades of blue sugarpaste together, cut in half then roll out.*

b *Cut out the pastillage fins, place on grey modelling paste and cut around them.*

Short cuts

⏱ You can use a ready-made cake and omit the freezing stage.

⏱ Make the fins from thick modelling paste only (but beware, they may flop in damp weather conditions).

⏱ If time is against you, try this alternative shark. The decoration (Stage Four) has been omitted to leave a smooth, grey finish and the board has been left with a plain sugarpaste covering.

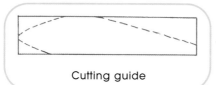

Cutting guide

STAGE TWO

 4 **Freezing the cake** Level the cake and remove the crust from the base. Then, in order to make it easier to carve, freeze the cake until it is firm (preferably overnight).

5 **Covering the fins** Knead the grey modelling paste until warm – adding a small amount of white vegetable fat if it feels stiff – then roll it out thinly. Place one of the dried pastillage fins on the paste and cut around the fin approximately 2mm (¹⁄₁₆in) from the edge (see picture **b**, page 30). Repeat to make the second side of the fin. Stick the two grey sides onto the pastillage fin then pinch the edges together – the join should disappear. Place to one side and repeat for the other fins and tail. Allow to dry.

STAGE THREE

6 **Carving the cake** Place the large body template on top of the frozen cake and, with a large knife, cut vertically through the cake along the lines of the template (see picture **c**). Cut the extra tail section from one of the off-cuts. Start to shape the shark by cutting his profile (see cutting guide). Then curve all the edges of the body to create the characteristic shark shape (see picture **d**). Once you are happy with the shark's body, transfer him onto waxed paper, securing his tail in place with a small amount of buttercream.

7 **Covering the shark** Spread a thin layer of buttercream over the cake to stick the sugarpaste. Roll out the grey sugarpaste and cover the cake. To take away the excess paste at the front, cut out a triangle of paste at the shark's snout and wrap the remaining paste under the head, smoothing the join closed. Ease the paste under the shark all around his body, then trim away the excess. Press a dresden tool into the soft paste to create the gill slits, the nostrils and the mouth.

8 **Attaching the fins and tail** Insert the individual fins and the tail in position, as indicated on the body template. Conceal the areas where the fins and the tail join the shark's body by painting the joins with 'let down'

c *Hold the template in place with pins and cut around it to form the shark's body.*

d *Carefully use the knife to curve all the edges of the shark's body.*

e *Using a fine paintbrush dipped in diluted black paste colour, apply the shark's stripes.*

grey sugarpaste (this is sugarpaste mixed with water until it becomes a thick smooth paste). Neaten any uneven paste with a damp brush as necessary. Leave and allow to dry thoroughly.

STAGE FOUR

 Painting the shark details Dilute some black paste colour in clear spirit and, using a fine paintbrush, carefully paint black vertical lines over the shark's body (see picture e). Then, mix up a variety of blues by adding white dust colour to slightly diluted blue paste colours (the colours should be quite thick in consistency). Apply the resulting colours to the shark in sweeping brush strokes from the nose to the tail, starting with the lightest colours under the body and gradually changing to the darkest shade along the top of his back (see picture f). Apply some additional black stripes as desired, and then leave to dry.

STAGE FIVE

 Adding details Transfer the finished shark to the covered board. Model eyes and teeth from the remaining sugarpaste and attach them to the sides of the shark's head with sugar glue.

 Creating the water effect With a large paintbrush, apply piping gel to the board so that the blue becomes reflective and the colours are intensified: this creates the illusion of water. It's a good idea to pour some gel from its pot onto the board and paddle it with your brush to remove any lumps before spreading. Once the board is covered, run the brush through the gel to create ripples (see picture g).

Adding the ribbon Finally, attach a ribbon around the edge of the board. If you cannot find a ribbon of a suitable colour, you can dye one to match the board exactly. To do this, dilute some paste food colour in a small bowl and run the ribbon through the colour. Then, wearing plastic disposable gloves to prevent the colour staining your fingers, squeeze out the excess liquid (see picture h) and allow the ribbon to dry.

> ### TIP
>
> ★ *Clean plastic milk cartons make excellent templates. Cut up the carton and place a section over the template in the book. Draw over the template with a pen and then cut along the drawn lines with a pair of scissors. You will have a template that can be used again and again.*

f *Use a medium paintbrush to apply the shades of blue to the shark's body.*

g *Apply gel to the board and run a brush through it to create a rippled effect.*

h *You can use diluted blue paste colour to dye your ribbon to match the board.*

Suzie Strawberry

Very few people admit to not liking strawberries. They are often associated with special occasions, bobbing in a glass of champagne, swimming in cream at Wimbledon or simply plucked plump, succulent and juicy straight from the plant on a hot summer's day – delicious!

CAKE AND DECORATION

5 egg 20cm (8in) heart-shaped madeira cake (see page 11)

28cm (11in) round cake board

Sugarpaste (rolled fondant):
750g (1lb 10oz) red,
600g (1lb 5oz) green,
75g (3oz) white

Dark green, golden yellow, and black paste food colours

Half quantity of buttercream

Icing (confectioner's) sugar

Gum tragacanth

Sugar glue

White vegetable fat (shortening)

90cm (36in) green ribbon

EQUIPMENT

Large carving knife

Ball tool (optional)

2.5mm (⅛ in) spacers – barbecue skewers work very well

Cutting wheel or knife

Non-stick work board

Smoother (optional)

Strawberry templates (see page 92)

Greaseproof (wax) paper

Circle cutters (optional):
2.5cm (1in) and 3.5cm (1⅜ in)

Large paintbrush

STAGE ONE

1 **Covering the board** Roll out the green sugarpaste (rolled fondant), using icing (confectioner's) sugar to prevent it sticking, and cover the board. Trim the edges flush with the board. Keep the trimmings. Leave to dry.

2 **Mixing the pastes** Add dark green paste colour and 2.5ml (½ teaspoon) gum tragacanth to 100g (3½ oz) of the green sugarpaste trimmings to make dark green modelling paste. Colour 25g (1oz) of the white sugarpaste yellow. Add 1.25ml (¼ teaspoon) gum tragacanth to the remaining white sugarpaste to make modelling paste, then colour half of it black.

STAGE TWO

3 **Carving the cake** Level the top of the cake and trim the crust from the base. Using a sharp knife, carefully cut away the cake towards the point to form the tip of the strawberry (see cutting guide). Next, carve away the sides of the cake by cutting a gentle curve from the centre of the cake down to all the lower edges to form a rounded shape (see picture **a**).

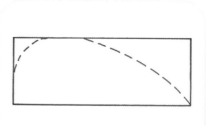

Cutting guide

a *Trim the crust from the base of the cake and round the top of the cake with a knife.*

Short cuts

⏱ The cake can easily be covered and decorated at the same time.

⏱ Omit the face details and leave as a plain strawberry.

⏱ Leave out the optional final stage of adding the shine.

 Covering the cake Place the cake on the cake board and cover it with a thin layer of buttercream. Roll out the red sugarpaste and cover the cake (see page 12). Trim away the excess paste. With a ball tool or a finger, indent the surface of the strawberry leaving the face area smooth. To make the seeds, roll small balls of yellow sugarpaste, elongate them into teardrops and attach them in the indentations using sugar glue (see picture ⓑ).

STAGE THREE

5 **Attaching the calyx and stem** Roll out the dark green modelling paste between 2.5mm (⅛in) spacers and cut 10cm (4in) long leaf shapes using a cutting wheel or small knife (see picture ⓒ). Attach these to the top of the strawberry to form the calyx. For the stem, roll a 2cm x 5cm (¾in x 2in) cylinder and glue in place.

6 **Making the eyes** Trace the template onto greaseproof (wax) paper. Cut out the whites of the eyes from thinly rolled white modelling paste and, using either the eye template or a 3.5cm (1⅜in) circle cutter, cut out the eye shapes. Cut the pupils from thinly rolled black paste using either the 2.5cm (1in) cutter or the template. Stick the whites and pupils in position on the cake, smoothing all the cut edges with your finger (see picture ⓓ). Add light spots by rolling two small balls of white paste and pressing them into each pupil.

7 **Making the nose and mouth** Roll a 1.5cm (⅝in) ball of red sugarpaste and attach it to the strawberry to form the nose. To make the mouth roll a long sausage of black modelling paste using a smoother to keep the paste even. Once the paste is thin enough, attach to the face as indicated on the template. Thinly roll out small sections of black paste and attach as cheeks and eyelashes.

8 **Adding shine (optional)** Using a large paintbrush, thinly spread a layer of white vegetable fat (shortening) over the entire surface of the strawberry. This will intensify the colour and give a good shine.

Use a paintbrush to apply white vegetable fat to the surface of the cake for shine.

ⓑ *Make small indentations for the seeds. Add the sugarpaste seeds to the indentations.*

ⓒ *Cut the calyx from rolled out dark green sugarpaste.*

ⓓ *Model the facial features and carefully attach them to the cake with sugar glue.*

Ballet Star

Ballet conjures up pretty images of tutus, ribbon laces and delicate figures. For this cake, however, I have used a slightly different interpretation using a bolder design to highlight a more contemporary approach. You could use the star cake as a basis for other decorative effects.

CAKE AND DECORATION

7 egg 25.5cm (10in) round madeira cake
(see page 11)

41cm (16in) round cake board

2.5kg (5lb 8oz) sugarpaste (rolled fondant)

Purple, cream and ruby red paste food colours

One quantity of buttercream

Gum tragacanth

Sugar glue

White vegetable fat (shortening)

1.2m (48in) purple ribbon

EQUIPMENT

Star templates (see page 93)

Carving knife

Non-stick work board

Textured rolling pin (HP)/ceramic veining tool (HP)

Paintbrush

Foam pieces

Circle cutter:
2.5cm (1in)

5-point calyx or star cutter

STAGE ONE

 Covering the board Colour 1.3kg (2lb 14oz) sugarpaste (rolled fondant) a rich purple. Roll it out and use it to cover the board. Place to one side to dry thoroughly.

 Colouring the pastes Colour 1.1kg (2lb 7oz) sugarpaste cream. Colour the remaining 100g (3½oz) white sugarpaste pink, kneading in 2.5ml (½ teaspoon) gum tragacanth to make pink modelling paste.

STAGE TWO

 Freezing the cake Remove the crust from the base of the cake. Level the top of the cake and place in a freezer. Freeze the cake until firm, preferably overnight.

STAGE THREE

 Carving the cake Make a paper template and place on top of the cake. Cut vertically through the cake along the edges of the template. Add a point to each arm of the star by using off-cuts, securing with buttercream. Cut from the centre of the star down to the tip of each point (see cutting guide). Mark a line along the centre of each arm and curve the edges by carving from this line down to the lower edge (see picture **a**). Transfer to the cake board.

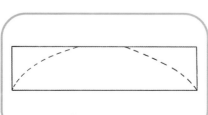

Cutting guide

a *Cut from the centre of the star to the end of each point then curve all the edges.*

5 **Covering the cake** Spread a thin layer of buttercream over the cake. Roll out the cream sugarpaste and cover the cake. Gently smooth the paste over the star and into the recesses being careful not to stretch it too much between the arms. Trim away the excess paste and put aside. Allow to dry.

STAGE FOUR

6 **Making the skirt** Score a line across the cake to mark the position of the waistband. Smear your work board with white vegetable fat (shortening) and roll out the pink modelling paste. Texture the paste with a textured rolling pin and cut into 6cm (2½in) wide strips (see picture **b**). Pleat one long edge of each strip, thin the pleated edge with a rolling pin and then cut the edge straight. Paint sugar glue along the scored line and place the skirt pieces in position, disguising any joins with folds in the paste. To make the waistband, cut a 6mm (¼in) wide strip from the modelling paste and attach it on top of the skirt. Use small pieces of foam to support the skirt as it dries (see picture **c**).

7 **Making the ballet shoes** Trace the shoe template onto paper or card and cut it out. Cut two shoes from thinly rolled pink modelling paste. Attach the shoes in position easing the paste to fit. To make the straps, cut thin strips from the pink modelling paste and secure (see picture **d**).

8 **Adding the face details** For the mouth, add some ruby paste colour to a small amount of pink modelling paste. Roll it into a thin sausage and cut to size using the template. Roll the cut ends and attach to the face. Model a small nose and glue in position. For the cheeks, lighten some of the pink modelling paste by adding cream sugarpaste. Thinly roll out the paste and cut two 2.5cm (1in) circles. Glue in position. For the eyelashes colour some pink modelling paste purple and roll into a thin sausage. Cut two lengths to size using the template. Roll the cut ends and attach to the face. Roll lashes and attach.

9 **Adding the finishing touches** Cut stars from rolled out cream sugarpaste, using a calyx or star cutter, and position them on the board. Attach the ribbon around the board with double-sided tape or non-toxic glue.

Short cuts

- Use ready-coloured paste.
- Make a plain skirt instead of a pleated one.
- Omit the small dancing stars.

TIP

★ *If your paste cracks as you cover the cake, add an additional piece of paste over the crack and blend it in with the heat of a finger; the join should disappear completely.*

Model the facial features and attach them to the cake with sugar glue.

b *Use a textured rolling pin to roll out the modelling paste then pleat the skirt.*

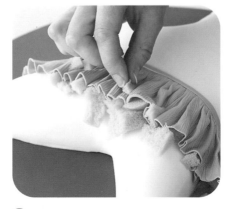

c *To keep the skirt in position as it dries, place pieces of foam above and below the folds.*

d *Cut thin modelling paste strips and carefully cross them over to make the ties.*

Carl Caterpillar

Caterpillars are often seen as pests as they munch their way through precious garden plants. However, these multi-legged creatures soon turn into much admired butterflies fluttering on the breeze. Carl Caterpillar has a charm all of his own and he's not letting go of that leaf!

CAKE AND DECORATION

7 egg 20cm (8in) square madeira cake (see page 11)

40cm x 35cm (16in x 14in) oval cake board

Sugarpaste (rolled fondant): 1.84kg (4lb 1oz) white, 200g (7oz) black

Icing (confectioner's) sugar

Green, yellow and black paste food colours

Sugar glue

Cabbage leaf (for veining)

Gum tragacanth

50g (2oz) pastillage

White vegetable fat (shortening)

One quantity of buttercream

Clear spirit, such as gin or vodka

140cm (55in) green ribbon

EQUIPMENT

Knives – large and small

Dresden tool

Caterpillar templates (see pages 92–93)

Non-stick work board

Sugar shaper (optional)

Dowel

Waxed paper

Circle cutters: 10cm (4in), 1.5cm (⅝in), 1cm (½in)

Large paintbrush

Natural sponge

STAGE ONE

1 **Covering the board** Thinly roll out a small amount of the black sugarpaste (rolled fondant), cut it into three pieces and stick sections to the board for the leaf areas. Colour 1.2kg (2lb 11oz) of the white sugarpaste light green and roll out using icing (confectioner's) sugar to prevent it sticking. Paint sugar glue or water over the uncovered surface of the board and cover the board with the sugarpaste. Remove the green sugarpaste from the black areas with a knife and texture the cut edge with a dresden tool to make teeth marks. Keep the trimmings to one side. Next, take a dry cabbage leaf and press the veins on the underside of the leaf into the soft paste (see picture). Repeat this process, positioning the veins to create the illusion of one large leaf. Allow to dry.

2 **Mixing the pastes** Add gum tragacanth to the remaining black sugarpaste – 5ml (1 teaspoon) gum to 225g (8oz) of sugarpaste. Add the light green board trimmings to the remaining white sugarpaste and colour it all a slightly darker shade of green than the board.

3 **Making the antennae** Trace two antennae templates onto paper. Colour the pastillage black, knead in a little white vegetable fat (shortening) and place in a sugar shaper with a large round disc. Squeeze the pastillage onto the templates (see picture **b**) and cut to size. Allow to dry.

a *Press a fresh cabbage leaf into the green sugarpaste to create the veins of the leaf.*

b *Use a sugar shaper to squeeze out two even black pastillage antennae.*

Short cuts

⏱ You could use a ready-baked cake.

⏱ Place the caterpillar's head at the end of its body rather than on top.

⏱ Use liquorice for the antennae.

⏱ Omit the painting stages.

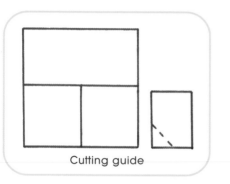

Cutting guide

STAGE TWO

4 **Freezing the cake** Level the cake and remove the crusts. Cut the cake in half, and then cut one portion in half again (see the cutting guide). Place the cake in the freezer.

STAGE THREE

5 **Carving the cake** Trace the body template onto paper and cut it out. Spread buttercream over one vertical end of the long cake and position one smaller cake onto the buttercream. Place the template on top of the cake and cut vertically down around the template. Remove the template, mark the top central line and curve all the sections of the body, removing a little cake at a time until the desired shape is achieved. Then, at the front end, cut away a diagonal slice from the top of the body section down to a height of 3cm (1¼in) as indicated on the carving template.

6 **Making the head** Cut out a 10cm (4in) card circle and place it on top of the remaining square cake and cut vertically down around the circle. Cut away a slice, as shown (see cutting guide), to enable the head to sit on the body. Mark the centre of the face, then round all the edges to create a rounded face. To secure the head, spread a thin layer of buttercream onto the cut away section of the body, insert a dowel cut to 11cm (4½in) at a slight angle and position the head securely (see picture **c**).

7 **Covering the cake** Place the cake on waxed paper and cover with a thin layer of buttercream. Roll out the green sugarpaste and cover the caterpillar. Ease the paste into position around the neck, between each section and under the body. Smooth the paste with the heat of your hand (see picture **d**) and trim away the excess, being careful not to take too much paste away. Place to one side to dry.

c *Attach the caterpillar's head to its body with a dowel to make it secure.*

d *Use your fingers to smooth the surface of the sugarpaste gently for an even finish.*

e *Apply diluted green paste colour with a large paintbrush to highlight the leaf detail.*

STAGE FOUR (OPTIONAL)

 8 **Painting the board and cake** Slightly dilute some light green paste colour in clear spirit, load a large paintbrush and paint the board (see picture (e)). The paste colour highlights the veining and brings the leaf to life. Mix up a range of greens ranging from a lime green to a blue green. Take a damp natural sponge and sponge the colours over the caterpillar, overlapping the colours so that they blend (see picture (f)). Allow to dry.

STAGE FIVE

9 **Securing the cake** Once the paint has dried, you can transfer the cake to the cake board and secure it in place on top of the cabbage leaf using sugar glue.

10 **Making the feet** Roll ten 2.5cm (1in) wide black modelling paste balls. Roll each ball into a cone shape and attach to the cake, smoothing it into shape with your finger. Add a 1.5cm (⅝in) wide black circle to the body above each foot (see picture (g)).

11 **Making the face** Cut out the eyes using the circle cutters and the black and white pastes and attach, smoothing the cut edges with your finger. Model the nose and cheeks from the green sugarpaste trimmings and make the smile and eyebrows from thinly rolled black paste (see picture (h)).

12 **Applying the finishing touches** Insert the antennae in position on top of the caterpillar's head. Place some black paste around the base of each antenna and carefully smooth them into flat, rounded shapes. Roll two 2cm (¾in) wide green balls and attach to the top of each antenna. Finally, paint all the unpainted green paste and then attach a ribbon around the board with non-toxic glue.

(f) *Blend shades of green over the caterpillar with a natural sponge for a vibrant effect.*

(g) *Make the feet and body spots from black modelling paste and attach them.*

(h) *The caterpillar's face is modelled from the black, white and green pastes.*

Cosy Coupé

Beep beep! Few children would be without a cosy coupé! Girls and boys alike will be thrilled to have this cake at their party. The colouring is very easily adapted: you can try pink or blue, or any combination of your own choice to suit the birthday girl or boy.

CAKE AND DECORATION

10 egg 20cm x 30cm (8in x 12in) madeira cake – a multisize cake pan is ideal (see page 11)

28cm (11in) petal-shaped cake board

Sugarpaste (rolled fondant): 1.865kg (4lb 2oz) white 100g (4oz) black

Purple, pink and orange paste food colours

Gum tragacanth

Half quantity of buttercream

Sugar glue

Edible black pen

90cm (36in) pink ribbon

EQUIPMENT

Coupé template (see page 92)

Large carving knife

Circle cutters: 5cm (2in) 4.25cm (1⅝in)

Waxed paper

Smoother

Non-stick work board

2mm (¹⁄₁₆in) spacers – (e.g. thick card)

Cutting wheel/knife

Flower cutters

Sugar shaper for optional trim

STAGE ONE

 Covering the board Colour 600g (1lb 5oz) of the sugarpaste (rolled fondant) purple. Roll it out and cover the board. Keep the trimmings to one side. Leave to dry.

 Colouring the pastes Colour 1kg (2lb 3oz) sugarpaste pale pink. Add 2.5ml (½ teaspoon) gum tragacanth to the black sugarpaste and 6.25ml (1¼ teaspoons) to the remaining white sugarpaste. Colour 225g (8oz) of the white paste dark pink, 25g (1oz) mid pink and 15g (½oz) orange. Add 2.5ml (½ teaspoon) gum tragacanth to 100g (3½oz) of the purple trimmings.

STAGE TWO

 Freezing the cake Level the cake and remove the crust from the base. Make two vertical cuts to make three 20cm x 10cm (8in x 4in) pieces. Stack the cakes using buttercream to stick each layer and then freeze.

STAGE THREE

 Carving the cake Pin the template to one side of the frozen cakes. Place the cakes so that the template is uppermost and cut around it (see picture **a**). Take a 5cm (2in) circle cutter and cut out the wheel arches. Cut away the base on each side to a depth of 1.5cm (⅝in) (see picture **b**).

a *Use a large carving knife to cut vertically around the template.*

b *Cut out wheel arches with a circle cutter and cut away the bottom to form a base.*

Short cuts

- ⏱ Use a ready-made cake.
- ⏱ Cover the car using one colour of sugarpaste only.
- ⏱ Simplify the decoration stage.
- ⏱ Omit the decorative trim.

Stand the car upright and narrow the top slightly by removing a thin tapering wedge from each side. Finally, curve the edges on all four corners of the car.

5 **Covering the underside of the car** Place the cake on its back on waxed paper. Spread a thin layer of buttercream over the base area of the car and the wheel arches. Cover this area using a 6cm (2½in) wide strip of purple paste. Smooth the paste into the wheel arches and trim flush with the sides of the car. Don't worry too much – most of this paste will be hidden.

6 **Covering the car** Reposition the car upright on the waxed paper. Spread a thin layer of buttercream over the remaining uncovered madeira and cover with the pale pink sugarpaste. Pull up the excess paste at one corner of the car to form a pleat, cut this away and smooth the join closed. Carefully trim the paste around the wheel arches and the base of the car and smooth the cut edges with your finger. Take the smoother and smooth the surface (see picture), paying particular attention to the window area.

7 **Making the wheels** Roll out the black modelling paste to a depth of 1cm (½in) and cut out four wheels using the circle cutter. Decorate the centres of each wheel as shown and leave to dry (see picture).

STAGE FOUR

8 **Adding the lower colour** Transfer the cake to the board. Paint sugar glue over the area above the wheel arches. Roll out a strip of dark pink modelling paste between the spacers and cut to a width of 6cm (2½in) (see picture). Roll the paste up and unroll it around the car (see picture f). Cut out the door using the template and replace it with a mid pink one (see pictures g and h). Trim each wheel arch and mark the corners with a knife.

9 **Adding the upper colour** Roll out half the purple modelling paste between spacers and cut into a 6cm (2½in) wide strip. On one side of the car, position the strip so that it goes up the front and over to the back. Cut the paste to abut the dark pink body of the car and cut out the door.

c Use a smoother to create an even finish to the pale pink base colour of the car.

d Cut flower shapes from the pink and white modelling paste and attach to the wheels.

e Roll out the dark pink modelling paste between spacers to form an even strip.

Variation

If the pink and purple Cosy Coupé is not suitable for the child you have in mind, the colour combinations can easily be adapted. In this alternative version, bright blue replaces the dark pink and green is used in place of the purple. A different colour has been chosen for the roof, and a simple round cake board replaces the petal board.

There is plenty of scope for varying the details. Here, the door has been kept the same colour as the lower part of the car – simply score around the door template to give the definition. The red and yellow 'go faster' stripes are made from rolled modelling paste and attached with sugar glue. The wheel decoration has also been simplified.

Repeat for the other side. Cut a rectangle of purple paste for the front, glue in place and mark the grill.

 10 **Adding details** Add mid pink paste to the front of the car below the windscreen and make two mid pink number plates. Cut a dark pink rectangle to fit the roof and glue in place. Make flowers from thinly rolled modelling paste and use to decorate the car and board.

 11 **Attaching the wheels** Attach the wheels to the car, then trim the car with dark pink modelling paste using a sugar shaper fitted with a small round disc. You may need to soften the paste first (see Tip).

 12 **Applying the finishing touches** Using a food pen, write an appropriate registration number on each of the number plates and attach your chosen ribbon around the board.

f *Unroll the dark pink strip of modelling paste around the bottom of the car.*

g *Use a cutting wheel or knife to cut around the door shape template. Remove the piece.*

h *Replace the door piece with a new door made from the mid pink modelling paste.*

Wilbur Walrus

Wilbur may look huge and ungainly, but he is brilliantly adapted to his Arctic environment. During the winter and spring, walruses spend much of their time drifting along on large floating fields of ice – Wilbur has brought his with him. Like his fellow walruses, he's very sociable!

CAKE AND DECORATION

8 egg 23cm (9in) square madeira cake (see page 11)

28cm (11in) round cake board

One quantity of buttercream

1.4kg (3lb) white sugarpaste (rolled fondant)

Brown, blue, black and yellow paste food colours

Sugar glue

Clear spirit, such as gin or vodka

Gum tragacanth

Snowflake dust

Piping gel

90cm (36in) blue ribbon

EQUIPMENT

Walrus templates (see page 93)

Carving knives, large and small

Rolling pin

A ruler or a smoother

Waxed paper

Dresden tool

Ball tool

Cocktail stick (toothpick)

Paintbrushes

STAGE ONE

1 **Freezing the cake** Level the cake and remove the crust. Cut the cake vertically in half and stack the two halves, placing a layer of buttercream between them to stick them together. Freeze the cake until firm (preferably overnight).

STAGE TWO

2 **Carving the walrus** Make a paper template, then remove the cake from the freezer and place the template against one long side of the cake. Carefully cut around the template with the carving knife to give the profile of the walrus. Place the cake trimmings to one side – these will be needed later to make the floating ice. Next, cut the walrus into a teardrop shape by cutting vertically down through the cake (the tip of the teardrop is at the tail end). Mark a midline on the top of the cake and carefully round the edges of the cake by carving from this line to create the body. Carve away the front of the walrus at an angle. Then, create the head by cutting down from the midline to the nostrils – use the template to locate these. Cut away the cake around the head to create a neck, then round off all the cut edges (see picture ⓐ). If you make a mistake, you can adjust the finished shape of the cake by adding pieces of sugarpaste (rolled fondant) before covering.

ⓐ *Gradually carve away the cake around the head to create a neck.*

ⓑ *Use the flat edge of a smoother or a ruler to give sharp edges to the block of ice.*

Short cuts

⏱ Use a ready-made cake.

⏱ Cover the whole of the cake board with the white sugarpaste ice, thus omitting the sea.

⏱ Omit the painting stage and leave the walrus as a smooth, flat colour.

 Carving the ice Take the cake trimmings and slice them horizontally to a depth of 2cm (¾in). Arrange the slices on the board to form a flat area for the walrus to sit on. Leave some areas of the edge clear.

 Covering the ice Spread a thin layer of buttercream over the cake trimmings and cover with white sugarpaste. Trim away the excess paste then gently press into the sides of the ice block with a smoother or the flat edge of a ruler (see picture ⓑ, page 48). Add 1.25ml (¼ teaspoon) gum tragacanth to 50g (2oz) of the trimmings to make white modelling paste.

 Making the sea Colour 200g (7oz) of the remaining sugarpaste blue. Paint sugar glue over the uncovered parts of the board. Roll out the blue paste and cut it into strips. Place these up against the ice flow (see picture ⓒ). Smooth the joins closed, and trim to fit the board. Leave to dry.

 Covering the walrus Colour the remaining sugarpaste pale brown. Place the walrus on waxed paper and cover with a layer of buttercream. Roll out the pale brown sugarpaste and cover the walrus, smoothing the paste carefully with your hand and trimming away the excess at the base. Keep the trimmings to one side. Take a dresden tool and press and drag it firmly through the sugarpaste to create his wrinkles and mouth (see picture ⓓ).

Making the face For the nostrils, eyes and tusk holes, press a ball tool into the soft paste in the appropriate places (see picture ⓔ). Finally, use a cocktail stick (toothpick) to make holes for his whiskers. Leave to dry.

STAGE THREE

Painting the walrus Separately, slightly dilute the brown, black and yellow paste colours in clear spirit. Using a small brush, paint a section of the walrus's wrinkles with dark browns and blacks (see picture ⓕ). Using a larger brush, paint over this section with darker colours at the base changing to lighter ones over the top of his back. Continue until the walrus is completely painted. Allow to dry.

ⓒ *Position strips of blue sugarpaste next to the edges of the ice block to form the sea.*

ⓓ *Use a dresden tool to create wrinkles by dragging it firmly through the paste.*

ⓔ *Press a ball tool into the sugarpaste to make indentations for the eyes.*

STAGE FOUR

 9 **Securing the cake** Once the paint has dried, carefully transfer the walrus to his floating ice platform and secure him in place with some sugar glue.

 10 **Making the rear flippers** Make two 2cm (¾in) wide sausages of pale brown sugarpaste for the rear flippers. Flatten each sausage, thin one end and attach the thinned end to the rear of the walrus. Cut the other ends flush with the underside of the cake, to look as if the walrus is sitting on his back flippers.

11 **Making the front flippers** For the front flippers, make a template then roll out the remaining pale brown sugarpaste to a depth of 3mm (⅛in). Cut out two mirror images from the paste then cut grooves into the paste to form 'fingers' (see picture g). Pinch the tips of each finger and smooth the cut edges. Place in position on the ice flow up against the walrus's body. Next, roll two 2.5cm (1in) wide balls of pale brown paste, flatten and position on top of each front flipper. Create wrinkles as before. Slide some waxed paper under the flippers to avoid painting the ice and paint as before. Carefully remove the waxed paper.

12 **Preparing the tusks** Roll the white modelling paste into a sausage the same width as the tusk holes. Roll one end to a point, cut to 4cm (1½in) in length and roll the cut end so it will fit snugly into the hole. Place sugar glue into the hole and position the tusk. Repeat for the other tusk.

 13 **Making the eyes** Roll small balls of white modelling paste and attach them in place. Colour some modelling paste black and add pupils and then position white 'light' spots.

 14 **Finishing touches** Dust the ice with snowflake dust to make the surface sparkle. Paint piping gel over the sea (see picture h) and finally, attach a ribbon around the board with non-toxic glue.

f Paint several diluted shades of brown, black and yellow over the walrus's body.

g Make the front and rear flippers from the pale brown sugarpaste, then paint as before.

h Use a paintbrush to apply piping gel over the sea to create a shiny rippled effect.

Party Bag

Evening bags are always popular and the beading on this one adds a wonderful touch of glamour. This cake has endless possibilities; you can change the look simply by changing the colour and decoration depending on the occasion or the young lady receiving the cake.

CAKE AND DECORATION

6 egg 20cm (8in) square madeira cake (see page 11)

28cm (11in) round cake board

1.3kg (2lb 14oz) sugarpaste (rolled fondant)

Paste food colours – blue and green to make turquoise; yellow and brown to make gold

Sugar glue

Gold and turquoise dragées

Half quantity of buttercream

White vegetable fat (shortening)

Light gold dust colour (SK)

90cm (36in) decorative ribbon(s)

EQUIPMENT

Set square

Carving knives

Waxed paper

Smoother

Two different widths of drinking straws

Cocktail stick (toothpick)

Ball tool

Ruler

Circle cutters:
2.5cm (1in) and 3.5cm (1½in)

Sugar shaper for optional trim

Paintbrushes

STAGE ONE

 Covering the board Colour 500g (1lb 2oz) sugarpaste (rolled fondant) turquoise to match the dragées. Roll out the paste and cover the board, trimming the sugarpaste flush with the edge. Place to one side to dry.

STAGE TWO

2 **Preparing the cake** Level the cake and remove the crust. Cut the cake in half vertically then spread a thin layer of buttercream over the top of one half and stack the other on top. Freeze until firm, preferably overnight.

STAGE THREE

3 **Carving the cake** Cut the stacked frozen cake to an overall length of 17cm (6¾in). Mark the centre line on each narrow side and along the top of the cake, using a set square to ensure the side lines are vertical. Mark 1cm (½in) either side of the top line. Take a large carving knife and cut diagonally down from each of these outer lines to the outer edges of the base of the cake to form the basic shape of the bag (see the cutting guide). Take a smaller knife and cut away two tapering diagonal sections at each end of the cake to a depth of 1cm (½in) (see picture). Then, place the cake on waxed paper.

a *Cut diagonally from the top line down to the bottom outer edges of the cake.*

Cutting guide

Short cuts

⏱ Use ready-coloured sugarpaste instead of colouring your own.

⏱ Use a ready-baked cake.

⏱ Simplify or omit the trim stage.

⏱ Omit the gold dusting and leave as a flat colour.

⏱ You can reduce the decoration time by finishing the cake at the end of Step 10. The pattern is in place and has been dusted but there are no beads.

4 **Covering the cake** Colour the white sugarpaste golden yellow to match your gold dust colour. Spread a thin layer of buttercream over one end of the cake to stick the sugarpaste. Roll out some of the golden yellow sugarpaste and cut one edge straight (see picture b). Place the straight edge at the base of the buttercreamed end of the cake and ease the paste into position on the side. Take a knife and cut the paste flush with the sides and top of the cake (see picture c). Repeat for the other end. Next, spread a layer of buttercream over one long side of the cake. Roll out the sugarpaste and cut one edge straight. Cover, smooth and trim as for the ends.

5 **Making the top decoration** To decorate, take a large drinking straw and cut across it diagonally with a pair of scissors to form an oval end. Press this oval end into the soft sugarpaste in a line along the top of the side – practise on an offcut of sugarpaste first (see picture d). Next create a line of upright ovals under the first line. Use the smaller drinking straw to press circles into the centre of each oval (see main photograph), and mark the centre of each circle with a cocktail stick (toothpick). Create a line of small round hollows with the small end of a ball tool then mark lines by pressing a ruler into the paste.

6 **Making the main pattern** Start by holding one of the circle cutters at an angle and press it randomly into the paste. Then, swap to the other cutter and make more curves. Next, use the oval drinking straw to indent 'S'-shaped patterns around the circles, and make 'C'-shaped patterns with the round drinking straw. Mark the centre of each circle with the cocktail stick as before. Finally, make random small hollow impressions in the paste with the small end of a ball tool. Once you are happy with your pattern, cover, texture and pattern the other side of the cake in the same way.

7 **Making the top of the bag** Cover the top of the cake with a thin layer of buttercream. Roll out the remaining golden yellow sugarpaste and cut it into a 3cm (1¼in) wide strip. Cut this strip to the length of your bag and place in position. Smooth the cut edges with a finger to give curved edges and press a straight edge down the centre of the strip to represent the opening.

b *Roll out the sugarpaste. Line up the straight edge with the bottom edge of the cake.*

c *Place the sugarpaste over each end of the bag and trim it flush with the edges.*

d *Practise patterns with the drinking straws, a cocktail stick, a ball tool and circle cutters.*

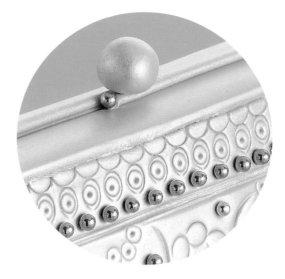

8 Adding the trim (optional) Soften some of the sugarpaste trimmings by kneading in some white vegetable fat (shortening) and a drop or two of boiled water. Then, place the paste in a sugar shaper together with a half moon disc. Squeeze out a length of paste and place it over one of the joins where the sides meet the end. Repeat for the other joins. Change the disc in the shaper to the small round one and squeeze out lengths to cover the join between the trim just applied and the sides of the bag. Then replace the disc with the medium round one and squeeze out lengths for the clasp on the top of the bag.

9 Making the handle To make the handle use the small rope disc and squeeze out a 30cm (12in) length (see picture e); twist this and place on the bag. Finally, roll a 2cm (¾in) wide ball and place on top of the bag for the clasp. Allow to dry.

STAGE FOUR

10 Dusting with gold Apply a thin layer of white vegetable fat over the entire surface of the bag using a large paintbrush: this will help the gold dust stick to the surface of the bag. Then, take a soft paintbrush and dip it carefully into the light gold dust and brush it onto the surface of the bag (see picture f). Continue until the whole bag is covered with gold dust and a good shine has been created.

11 Adding the beads Mix a little of the sugarpaste trimming with a small amount of boiled water to make a thick glue. Use a paintbrush to place a little of the glue in each ball tool impression then carefully pick up the dragées and place in the hollows (see picture g). NOTE: Dragées tarnish very quickly in even a slightly moist atmosphere, so be sure to store your finished cake in a dry place.

12 Assembling the cake Carefully transfer the finished party bag cake to the cake board. Finally, attach your chosen ribbons around the edge of the board.

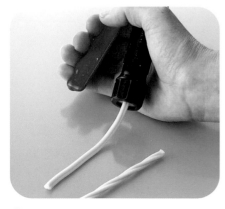

 Using a sugar shaper and a small rope disc, squeeze out a length of paste for the handle.

f *Use a paintbrush to apply light gold dust to the textured sugarpaste.*

g *Carefully stick the dragées into the indentations using a thick glue.*

Skippy Birthday

Getting tangled up in a skipping rope whilst trying to work out how to actually turn the rope and jump over it at the same time is all part of the fun. Skipping is good exercise and, once you've mastered the basic technique, it's so easy!

CAKE AND DECORATION

6 egg madeira cake baked in 23cm x13cm (9in x 5in) tin (a multisize cake pan is ideal) and a 8cm (3⅛in) round food can (see page 11)

40cm x 35cm (16in x 14in) oval cake board

Sugarpaste (rolled fondant): 2kg (4lb 6oz) white and 50g (2oz) black

Paste food colours: lime green, ruby/rose (to make pink), brown, orange, purple and yellow

Half quantity of buttercream

Gum tragacanth

White vegetable fat (shortening)

Sugar glue

140cm (55in) pink ribbon

EQUIPMENT

Carving knife

Waxed paper

Rolling pin

Non-stick work board

Sugar shaper

Craft knife

Paintbrushes

2mm (¹⁄₁₆in) spacers (thick card works well)

Zigzag cutter (FMM)

Flower cutters

Small circle cutters

STAGE ONE

Colouring the paste Colour 1.2kg (2lb10oz) of the white sugarpaste (rolled fondant) green, roll it out and cover the board. Colour 525g (1lb 2oz) sugarpaste pale pink and 200g (7oz) flesh colour (using brown, orange and a touch of ruby).

STAGE TWO

Preparing the cakes Level the rectangular cake and remove the crusts. Cut in half diagonally (see cutting guide). Turn one half over and secure the halves together with buttercream to make a triangle. Remove the top 2.5cm (1in) of the triangle to make the neck. Level the small cake to a height of 4cm (1½in) and remove the crusts. Freeze both cakes until firm.

STAGE THREE

Carving the cakes Mark a curve on the base of the triangular cake and cut away from the centre to the edges along the curve. Reduce the height of the narrow end to 2cm (¾in) by slicing up from the neck to the lower edge of the dress. Carve the top of the small cake to make a round face.

Covering the cakes Place both the cakes on waxed paper. Spread a thin layer of buttercream over the top of the dress cake only (see picture).

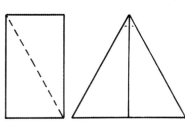
Cutting guide

a *Spread a thin layer of buttercream over the larger cake, leaving out the vertical base.*

Roll out the pale pink paste and use a rolling pin to lift it onto the cake (see picture **b**). Trim away the excess paste from around the sides and neck and cut the paste flush with the base of the dress (see picture **c**). Colour 225g (8oz) of the pale pink trimmings a deep pink. Spread buttercream over the base of the dress. Then roll out the deep pink sugarpaste and cut one edge straight. Cover the base of the dress by placing the straight edge against the board, then smooth and cut the paste flush with the dress. Spread a thin layer of buttercream over the head cake then roll out the flesh-coloured sugarpaste and use to cover the small cake. Cut away the excess paste, then smooth and polish the face with your hand. Allow to dry.

5 **Mixing the modelling paste** Colour 50g (2oz) of the sugarpaste trimmings mid pink, then colour the same amount purple. Next, knead in 1.25ml (¼ teaspoon) gum tragacanth to each. Also, knead in 1.25ml (¼ teaspoon) gum into 50g (2oz) each of deep pink, white and black sugarpaste. Colour the remaining 25g (1oz) white sugarpaste yellow and add a pinch of gum. Allow the gum to take effect.

STAGE FOUR

6 **Decorating the face** Transfer both cakes to the covered board and secure in place. Soften a small amount of the mid pink modelling paste by adding white vegetable fat (shortening) and a drop or two of boiled water and knead until malleable (rather like chewing gum). Roll into a thick sausage and place in the sugar shaper together with the small round disc. Pump the shaper and squeeze out a length onto your work board. Leave it to air dry for a few minutes, then take a craft knife and cut two 1cm (½in) lengths and a 4cm (1½in) length. Next, with a fine paintbrush, paint a smile of sugar glue on the girl's face and position the cut pieces, adjusting as necessary. Model a small ball nose from purple modelling paste and glue in place. Soften the black modelling paste, as described above, and place in the sugar shaper. Pump and squeeze out a length as before. Dry for a few minutes then cut two 1cm (½in) lengths, curve each length and glue in place for eyes.

b *Carefully lift the rolled out sugarpaste onto the triangular cake.*

c *Trim the pale pink paste along the edge of the dress cake. Keep the trimmings.*

d *Roll each strand of hair to a rounded point with your finger.*

7 **Making the hair** Replace the disc in the sugar shaper with the medium round one. Squeeze out eight lengths of black modelling paste directly onto the covered board for the strands of flying hair . Cut each strand to size with a diagonal cut, then arrange as required and glue in place. Squeeze out approximately 15 6cm (2⅜in) lengths of black paste onto your work board then roll one end of each length to a rounded point (see picture **d**). Paint sugar glue over the top of the head and arrange the hair into a fringe.

8 **Making the bows** Smear white vegetable fat over your work board then roll out some deep pink modelling paste and cut out two 12cm x 1.5cm (4¾in x ⅝in) and two 2cm x 1cm (¾in x ½in) strips. Paint some glue in the centre of each large strip and bring the ends into the centre (see picture **e**). Squeeze the centre of the bows slightly and wrap the smaller strips around these joins. Attach the bows in position (see picture **f**).

9 **Decorating the dress** Thinly roll out some mid pink modelling paste between spacers. Press a zigzag cutter into the paste and remove. Create 1cm (½in) wide zigzag strips by cutting straight lines on either side of the zigzag (see picture **g**). Glue the resulting strips to the neck and hemline of the dress. Continue to decorate the dress using strips, circles and simple flowers cut from modelling paste. The design can be as elaborate or as simple as you wish.

10 **Applying the finishing touches** Place some softened black modelling paste into the sugar shaper together with the large roll disc. Squeeze out lengths directly onto the board for the arms and legs. Bend the arms and one leg and cut each limb to size with a craft knife. For the hands and shoes, roll small balls of dark pink modelling paste, flatten and glue in place. Next, place some softened white modelling paste in the sugar shaper together with the medium round disc and squeeze out the skipping rope directly onto the board. Cut the rope away where it crosses the shoe and adjust the position of the rope as necessary. Cut the ends of the rope at an angle so that they can then be attached to each hand. Finally, attach a ribbon around the board.

e Roll out strips of deep pink modelling paste and fold over the ends to form the bows.

f Secure each bow at an angle, adjusting the loops and centre of the bow as desired.

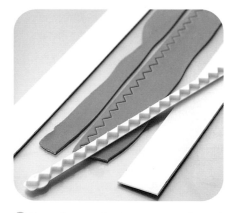

g Use a zigzag cutter to make the patterned stripes of the dress from modelling paste.

Bee Happy

At the first signs of warmer weather, bees arrive in the garden to help pollinate the flowers. As summer approaches, they get busy collecting nectar to make delicious honey. This buzzy, busy bee has found a wonderful flower and there's no sting in his tail!

CAKE AND DECORATION

6 egg 15cm (6in) ball-shaped madeira cake (see page 11)

38cm (15in) round cake board

2.2kg (4lb 13oz) sugarpaste (rolled fondant)

Orange, yellow, brown, olive and black paste food colours

White vegetable fat (shortening)

350g (12oz) pastillage

Powdered gelatine

Icing (confectioner's) sugar

Half quantity of buttercream

Gum tragacanth

Sugar glue

Clear spirit, such as gin or vodka

1.2m (47in) orange ribbon

EQUIPMENT

Empty toilet rolls

Waxed paper

Non-stick work board

2mm (1/16 in) cardboard spacers

Templates (see page 94)

Flexible plastic to make templates (such as the lid of a margarine or ice-cream tub)

Cutting wheel or knife

Plastic sleeve

Sugar shaper or garlic press

Piping tube (tip)

STAGE ONE

1 **Covering the board** Colour 1.2kg (2lb 10oz) of the sugarpaste (rolled fondant) deep orange. Roll it out and cover the cake board. Keep the trimmings. Allow to dry.

2 **Making the petals** Cover the toilet rolls with waxed paper to make formers. Make a petal template. Smear the work board with white vegetable fat (shortening) and roll out some pastillage between spacers. Place the template on the paste and cut around it. Leave the shape for a moment then turn it over and place on a former with the reverse side uppermost (see picture). Make 16 petals plus extras to allow for breakages. Allow to dry.

3 **Making the antennae** Colour a small amount of the pastillage black and roll into two 5cm (2in) lengths. Position each piece in a curve and allow to dry.

4 **Making the wings** Make the templates and place under waxed paper. Soak 5ml (1 teaspoon) powdered gelatine in 15ml (3 teaspoons) water with 2.5ml (½ teaspoon) icing (confectioner's) sugar. Dissolve over a pan of simmering water. Pour 5ml (1 teaspoon) of the liquid over each template (see picture). As the mixture sets, take a knife and cut radial lines. Allow to dry.

a Carefully turn the petal over onto the former. Do not move it until it is completely dry.

b Pour the gelatine mixture onto waxed paper. It can be trimmed later if necessary.

Short cuts

⏱ Make the centre of the flower all one colour.

⏱ Cover the back of the flower with one piece of smooth green sugarpaste before inserting the petals, or omit the calyx altogether.

⏱ Leave out the bee, make a simple butterfly or buy a ready-made insect instead.

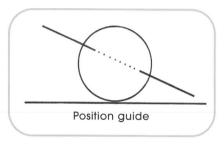

Position guide

STAGE TWO

 Covering the cake Remove the cake from its tin and take the crust off (see picture c). If the cake has been cooked in two halves, level them both and stick them together with buttercream. Colour 1kg (2lb 3oz) sugarpaste a deep yellow. Place the cake on waxed paper and cover with a layer of buttercream. Roll out the deep yellow sugarpaste and place over the cake, ease it around the base of the ball and pull up the excess to form a pleat. Cut this away, smooth the join and trim the excess. Keep the trimmings to one side. There is no need to smooth the sugarpaste because it will be covered later.

6 **Mixing the modelling paste** Add 3.75ml (¾ teaspoon) gum tragacanth to 150g (5oz) of both the yellow and orange sugarpaste trimmings to make modelling paste. Then colour as follows: 50g (2oz) golden brown, 25g (1oz) mid brown, 25g (1oz) very dark brown and the remainder dark olive.

STAGE THREE

7 **Preparing the position of the petals** Draw a line around the circum-ference of the cake to mark where the petals are to be inserted (see position guide). The angle of this line with the base will determine the overall angle of your flower, so experiment with the petals to see what you prefer. Transfer the cake to the board and position it so that the front petals will not protrude over the edge of the board.

8 **Adding the petals** Mix some of the yellow sugarpaste trimmings with a little boiled water to make a thick glue. Carefully insert a petal 2.5cm (1in) into the cake at the top of the scribed line – it should go into the cake fairly easily. Secure it in place with the thick yellow glue. Insert the next petal at the lowest point and then the other petals at equal distances between the first two petals.

9 **Making the flower centre** Mark the centre of the flower and a 12.5cm (5in) ring, then cover the entire area with sugar glue. Add some white vegetable fat and a little cooled boiled water to some of the yellow

c Allow the cake to cool, then remove from its tin and take off the crust.

d Use a sugar shaper or a garlic press to make tufts of sugarpaste for the flower centre.

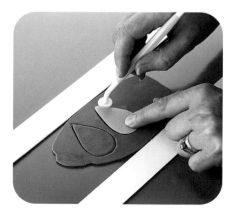

e Use a cutting wheel or knife to cut out shapes to form the calyx of the flower.

sugarpaste trimmings. Using either a sugar shaper fitted with a mesh disc or a garlic press, squeeze out small tufts of paste (see picture) and attach them around the outside of the flower up to the line of the marked ring. Soften some orange sugarpaste trimmings and roughly mix them with some softened yellow, then make tufts and attach them all around the edge of the marked circle. Continue with the yellow tufts until the centre is reached and finish off with the tufts of mixed paste.

10 **Making the calyx** Make a card or plastic template. Knead white vegetable fat into the olive modelling paste and roll it out between the spacers. Place the template on the paste and, using a cutting wheel or knife, cut around the template (see picture). Repeat until you have made enough shapes to cover the back of the flower. Using a cutter of a similar shape will help to speed up the process. Glue the shapes, pointed side uppermost, to the back of the flower in overlapping layers so that the points are visible between the petals.

11 **Making the bee's head** Model a 3cm (1¼in) ball from mid brown paste for the bee's head, and add a smile by pressing the wide end of a piping tube (tip) into the paste (see picture).

12 **Making the bee's body** Model the golden brown modelling paste into an 8cm (3in) long teardrop. Thinly roll out the dark brown paste, cut it into strips and attach to the body. Then texture the body with a cutting wheel or knife. For the legs, model six dark brown teardrops and attach them underneath the body (see picture).

13 **Adding the finishing touches** Make a nose and eyes from small pieces of golden brown, black and white modelling paste. Insert the antennae in position on the top of the head and add small balls of black paste to their tips. Glue the head to the body, insert the wings and attach the bee to the cake (see picture). Finally, attach a ribbon around the board with non-toxic glue.

TIPS

★ Collect 16 empty toilet rolls before you begin, so all the petals can be made together.

★ Inserting some uncooked dried spaghetti into the bee's body before attaching the head will help to keep it in place.

f Use the wide end of a piping tube to add the curve of the bee's smile.

g Assemble the bee from the gelatine wings and modelling paste head and body.

h Attach the bee in position on the tufted paste of the flower using sugar glue.

Clever Cat

Cunning and sly, this clever little cat likes to keep humans in step. Despite being a loner, he does love attention. A tickle under his chin will bring on a steam engine purring of satisfaction. He's so lifelike – he'd jump off that cake board at the first sign of a mouse!

CAKE AND DECORATION

8 egg madeira cake divided between 2 x 15cm (6in) round tins and a 10cm (4in) round tin (see page 11)

25.5 cm (10in) round cake board

White unbreakable 'gel (OP)

1.75kg (3lb 12oz) sugarpaste (rolled fondant)

Golden brown, green, black and brown paste food colours

One quantity of buttercream

70g (2¾oz) modelling paste

Sugar glue

Flesh dust colour

Clear spirit, such as gin or vodka

Piping gel (warmed)

EQUIPMENT

Palette knife

No.1 piping tube (tip)

Plastic sheet or bag

Cat templates (see page 94)

Pins

Dowel

Large carving knife

Waxed paper

Cutting wheel or craft knife

Dresden tool

Scissors

Scouring pad

Paintbrushes

STAGE ONE

 Making the whiskers (optional) Mix the unbreakable gel following the instructions on the pack. Mix with a palette knife until smooth. Using a no.1 piping tube (tip), pipe 8cm (3in) lines onto a plastic sheet: leave to dry.

 Covering the board Place the cake board on top of a smaller board or plate to lift it off the work surface. Colour 700g (1lb 7oz) of sugarpaste (rolled fondant) golden brown, roll it out and cover the board, bringing the paste over the edges. Trim the paste flush with the underside of the board. Leave to dry.

STAGE TWO

 Preparing the cakes Level the cakes and trim the crusts from their bases. Stack the cakes placing a layer of buttercream between each cake (see cutting guide). Insert a dowel for support and then freeze until firm.

STAGE THREE

Carving the cake Make two side profile templates and pin them to opposite sides of the cakes. Cut around the templates with a large knife, cutting from one template through to the other, to create the cat outline. Make the front profile template, pin in position and cut around it (see picture).

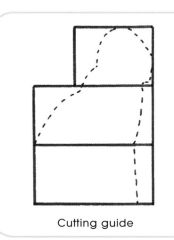

Cutting guide

a Carve the cake around the front template to create the cat's body shape.

Short cuts

⏱ If a white cat is appropriate, finish the cake at the end of step 11, omitting the painting. Alternatively, use ready-coloured sugarpaste.

Mark the position of the legs by holding the templates in place and cutting into the cake along the lines of the templates. Remove a tapered triangle of cake from between the front legs and then cut away the excess cake from the outer sides of the front legs back towards the hind legs. Curve the cut edges. Shape the back of the cat by cutting down from his backbone then round the neck. Cut away under the sides of the face. Shape the head and make the face by carving out eye sockets and shaping the chin. Leave the muzzle flat and then shape the cheeks. Once you are happy with the shape, place the cake on waxed paper.

5 **Covering the cake** Spread a layer of buttercream over the cake (see picture ⓑ) and then cover with white sugarpaste. Pull up any excess paste to form pleats, then cut these away and smooth the joins. Ease the paste under the neck, around the legs and under the body and trim to fit. Smooth the paste but do not worry too much about the finish, as the texturing will hide any imperfections. Take a cutting wheel and make a few marks over the cat to indicate the general direction of the fur. Cover the area you are not about to texture with cling film to prevent the sugarpaste from drying out. Then, run the wheel repeatedly over sections of the sugarpaste to make the fur.

6 **Making the paws** (see picture ⓒ) Make a 2.5cm (1in) wide ball of white sugarpaste, divide it in half and roll the two halves into balls. Flatten the balls slightly. Take the scissors and make three cuts to form four claws. Round the cut edges by rolling each claw between your fingers and mark a nail in each with a dresden tool. Slice away the back of the paws at an angle so they will fit snugly under the haunches. Glue in position. Texture small strips of white sugarpaste with the cutting wheel and attach above the paws to hide the join with the cat's body. Then make the front paws, but do not worry too much about these as they will be hidden by the tail.

7 **Making the tail** Take the sugarpaste trimmings and roll into a 30cm (12in) tapered sausage. Texture as before and then cut the wider end at a 45º angle and attach to the back of the cat. Blend the tail paste into the body and texture over the join. Position the tail around the cat.

ⓑ *Smooth a thin layer of buttercream over the entire cake before adding the sugarpaste.*

ⓒ *Make the front paws and small textured strips from white sugarpaste.*

ⓓ *Make the ears and the ear tufts from white modelling paste.*

8 **Making the ears** Make an ear template, then roll out the modelling paste to a thickness of 2.5mm (⅛in). Cut out two ears, one being the mirror image of the other (see picture d). Paint a line of sugar glue along the base of each ear and position on the cake. Leave to dry.

STAGE FOUR

 9 **Making the muzzle** Roll two 1.5cm (⅝in) balls of white sugarpaste and flatten slightly. Pinch one side of each to create circles with wedged profiles. Texture the whisker area with a scouring pad and then make indentations for the whiskers with a dresden tool. Then, make a 4cm (1½in) long cone of white sugarpaste. Pinch along opposite sides of the cone to flatten it and then pinch the base of the cone into a triangle before attaching it to the mouth (see picture e). Fix and smooth the muzzle onto the cat's face using sugar glue. Then texture the paste with the cutting wheel to disguise the join and make indents for the nostrils with a dresden tool.

10 **Making the eyes** Colour 10g (⅓oz) each of green and black modelling paste. Model the eyeballs and attach in position. Make the eyelids from black modelling paste and glue around the eyeball. Model some sugarpaste into two teardrop shapes, texture them and attach to the sides of the nose – bring them over the tops of the eyes to form the brow (see picture f).

11 **Finishing touches** Cut and texture two 1cm (⅜in) wide strips of white modelling paste and glue to the inside base of each ear. Cut and texture two 4cm (1½in) petal shapes from modelling paste and remove sections of paste from the petal shapes to give them a jagged appearance. Attach to the inside outer edges of each ear (see picture d). Insert the whiskers into the holes in the muzzle and trim so they are fractionally wider than the cat. Apply a little flesh dust colour onto the tip of the cat's nose and into the inside of the ears.

12 **Painting the fur (optional)** Dilute the paste colours in clear spirit and paint the textured fur. Once dry, transfer the cat to the board and add warm piping gel to the eye (see picture g).

Paint your desired coat pattern with a paintbrush and diluted paste food colours.

e *Make the muzzle from pieces of sugarpaste. Add holes for whiskers with the dresden tool.*

f *Use green and black modelling paste for the eyes and textured sugarpaste for the brows.*

g *Use a fine paintbrush to apply warm piping gel around the eyes.*

Space Shuttle

Space travel has long been of interest to humankind and regular trips to the moon are now a real possibility. If you know anyone who's fascinated by exploring the world of space travel, this space shuttle is fuelled and ready for boarding. We have lift-off!

CAKE AND DECORATION

6 egg 15cm (6in) ball-shaped madeira cake (see page 11)

25cm (10in) round cake board

1.675kg (3lb 11oz) sugarpaste (rolled fondant)

Dark blue, black and cream paste food colours

Gum tragacanth

White vegetable fat (shortening)

Half quantity of buttercream

75g (3oz) pastillage

White dust colour

Sugar glue

Clear spirit, such as gin or vodka

EQUIPMENT

Small board or plate

Shuttle templates (see page 94)

Waxed paper

Non-stick work board

Foam or kitchen paper

Ball tool

Small metal file

Craft knife or cutting wheel

Smoother

Black food pen

Natural sponge

Paintbrushes

Circle cutters:
2cm (¾in) and 1cm (½in)

STAGE ONE

1 **Covering the board** Place the cake board on top of an object such as a smaller board or plate so that you can lift it off your work surface. Colour 600g (1lb 5oz) sugarpaste (rolled fondant) dark blue, roll it out and cover the board bringing the paste over the edges. Trim the paste so it is flush with the underside of the board (see picture a). Place to one side to dry.

2 **Mixing the pastes** Colour 900g (2lb) sugarpaste a pale cream. Add 3.75ml (¾ teaspoon) gum tragacanth to 175g (6oz) white sugarpaste to make modelling paste. Take 25g (1oz) of the modelling paste and colour it black.

3 **Making the wings and tail** Trace the tail and wing templates onto waxed paper or card. Smear white vegetable fat (shortening) onto the work board and roll out a small amount of pastillage. Place the tail fin template on top of the pastillage, carefully cut it out and transfer to a flat porous surface, such as foam or kitchen paper, to dry. Colour the remaining pastillage black and roll it out. Place the wing template on the paste, cut it out and leave to dry thoroughly in the same way as the tail fin (see picture b).

a Trim the blue sugarpaste flush with the underside of the cake board.

b Use black pastillage for the wings and white pastillage for the tail fin – leave to dry.

STAGE TWO

4 **Covering the cake** Remove the crust from the cake (see picture **c**). If the cake has been cooked in two halves, level it and stick the two halves together with buttercream. Place the cake on waxed paper and cover it with a thin layer of buttercream to hold the sugarpaste. Next, roll out the cream-coloured sugarpaste and place over the cake. Ease the paste around the base of the ball and pull up the excess to form a pleat. Cut this away, smoothing the join and then trim the excess paste from the base of the cake. Keep the trimmings to one side. There is no need to smooth the sugarpaste. Using a ball tool, make a random pattern of craters of different sizes over the surface of the cake by pressing the tool repeatedly into the soft paste (see picture **d**). Move the ball tool in a circular motion around the outside of the craters and gently rub your finger over the indentations to soften their appearance.

5 **Modelling the shuttle** Ensure the pastillage wings and tail fin are dry, then gently file both pieces to remove any rough edges. Add a small amount of white vegetable fat into the modelling paste and work it until it is pliable. Roll 125g (4½oz) of paste into a 3.5cm (1⅜in) wide sausage (see picture **e**), shape one end into a cone (the nose of the shuttle) and cut the other at a slight angle to give an overall length of 15cm (6in). Place it on your work surface to flatten the base and smooth down the sides so they are at right angles to the base. Mark the cargo bay with a craft knife or cutting wheel and then glue the body into position on the black pastillage wings. Next, gently press on the top of the nose area with a finger to create the windscreen. Cut into the rear of the body with a craft knife and insert the vertical fin into position.

6 **Making the engines** To make the body for the manoeuvring engines, model two 1.5cm (⅝in) balls of white modelling paste into 3cm (1¼in) long cones. Flatten each cone on your work surface and vertically cut away both ends. Glue in position. To make the main engines, model 1.5cm (⅝in) balls of black modelling paste into cones, cut the wider ends flat, mark two rings around each engine with a craft knife or cutting wheel and glue in position. Make smaller cones for the manoeuvring engines and stick them in place.

c *Once the cake has cooled, take it out of its tin and remove the crust.*

d *Use a ball tool to create a pattern of craters on the moon's surface.*

e *Roll a sausage of modelling paste with a smoother to form the body of the shuttle.*

7 **Making the wings** Thinly roll out some white modelling paste and cut in half. Place one half over a pastillage wing so that it adjoins the body of the shuttle. With a craft knife or cutting wheel cut the paste 2mm (⅟₁₆in) in from the edge of the wing and remove the excess. Repeat for the other wing. Add thin triangles of black paste to the forefront of the wings (see picture **f**). Then position a half oval to the nose so that it adjoins the black pastillage on the base and comes slightly up the sides of the nose cone. Add the windscreen and other space shuttle markings with a black food pen (see picture **g**).

STAGE THREE

8 **Painting the cake** Mix white dust colour with cream and black colours to make pale cream and pale grey respectively. Slightly dilute each colour with clear spirit and, using a damp sponge, apply different colours to different areas of the moon starting at the base of the cake. Next, mix a dark grey and paint grey circles around the tops of the craters (see picture **h**). Stipple over the circles with a dry brush to soften the effect. Allow the paste colours to dry.

STAGE FOUR

9 **Adding the moon's face** For the nose, take some of the cream sugarpaste trimmings and roll into a small ball, elongate into a cone and position on the cake. For the mouth, colour some of the modelling paste trimmings a dark grey, roll into a small ball then elongate into a teardrop. Bend the end over slightly and glue in place. For the eyes, cut two 2cm (¾in) white circles from thinly rolled modelling paste and two 1cm (½in) circles from black modelling paste. Position the eyes and then add white 'light' spots to each. Roll eyebrows from light grey modelling paste and attach in position.

10 **Assembling the cake** Mix some cream sugarpaste trimmings with a little water to make a thick paste. Secure the cake to the board and the shuttle to the cake using this thick paste as a glue.

f *Cut out the shapes needed to decorate the fuselage and wings.*

g *Use a black food pen to add the windscreen and window details to the fuselage.*

h *Use a fine paintbrush to add grey highlights to the crater indentations.*

Lucky Ladybird

Ladybirds are always popular and very welcome in the garden. They appear as characters in many children's books and are also considered symbols of good luck. Maybe it is their bright red coats and black spots that make them so appealing.

CAKE AND DECORATION

5 egg madeira cake baked in a 1 litre (2 pint/5 cup) pudding basin and an 8cm (3in) food can (see page 11)

25cm (10in) round cake board

Sugarpaste (rolled fondant):
500g (1lb 2oz) green
700g (1lb 7oz) black
200g (7oz) red
75g (3oz) white

25g (1oz) pastillage

Yellow and black paste food colours

Half quantity of buttercream

Gum tragacanth

Sugar glue

80cm (32in) red, black and yellow ribbons

EQUIPMENT

Pan scourer

Ladybird template
(see page 91)

Smoother

Dowel

Circle cutters:
8cm (3in) for the base
3.5cm (1⅜in) for the spots
2cm (¾in) for the cheeks

Carving knife

Waxed paper

2.5mm (⅛in) spacers
(e.g. barbecue skewers or thick cardboard)

STAGE ONE

 Covering the board Roll out the green sugarpaste (rolled fondant) and cover the board. Take a clean pan scourer and press it into the soft sugarpaste to create the grass (see picture ⓐ). There are many types of scourers, so experiment to see which effect you like best. Once you are happy, trim the sugarpaste flush with the edges of the board and leave it to dry.

2 **Making the antennae** Trace two antenna templates onto paper. Colour the pastillage black and use a smoother to roll it into a long sausage. Cut it in half and place one half over each template, trim and allow to dry.

STAGE TWO

3 **Preparing the cakes** Level the bowl cake to 1.5cm (⅝in) above the level to which it has risen in the pudding basin and freeze both of the cakes until they are firm.

STAGE THREE

 Carving the cake Press an 8cm (3in) circle cutter into the centre of the levelled surface of the bowl cake to a depth of at least 2cm (¾in). Using a knife, cut horizontally towards the cutter at a depth of 1.5cm (⅝in) from the outside edges, to create the base. Remove the circle cutter.

ⓐ *Press a scourer into the surface of the sugarpaste to represent the grass.*

Cutting guide

Position guide

Short cuts

- Use ready-coloured pastes.

- Leave out the grass texture from the board.

- Cover the body with red sugarpaste rather than black and mark the join in the wings with a knife. Note: you will require 250g (9oz) black and 450g (1lb) red sugarpaste to cover the cake in this way.

- Use a fabric bow with wired edges.

- Use liquorice for the antennae.

Place the large cake on its base and gently round the cut edge between the base and the sides. Remove the remaining crust from the cakes. You may also need to adjust the shape of the ladybird's back to form more of a dome because pudding bowl shapes vary. Cut the small cake to a height of 5cm (2in). Mark the mid line around the circumference then carve from this line to the centre of both the top and base to create a flattened ball shape (see cutting guide, page 73, and picture **b**).

5 **Covering the cake** Spread a layer of buttercream on the underside of the ladybird (not the base) to hold the sugarpaste. Roll out the black sugarpaste and cut a 4cm (1½in) wide strip. Place the cake in the palm of your hand and wrap the black sugarpaste strip around the underside (see picture **c**). Cut the paste flush with the base and place the cake upright on waxed paper. Smooth the cut edge. Spread buttercream over the top of the ladybird and cover with black sugarpaste. Cut the paste flush with the underside and smooth away the join. Spread buttercream over the head and cover with black sugarpaste, gather the excess paste at the back of the head and cut it off. Insert the dowel into the body of the ladybird and position the head by pushing it onto the dowel (see position guide, page 73). Blend the join and leave to dry.

6 **Mixing modelling paste** Add 5ml (1 teaspoon) gum tragacanth to the red sugarpaste. Weigh the black trimmings and add gum tragacanth to them – 5ml (1 teaspoon) to 225g (8oz). Colour 25g (1oz) sugarpaste deep yellow and add 1.25ml (¼ teaspoon) gum tragacanth. (Note: the amount of gum needed for the yellow is greater than normal because, to achieve such a deep shade, a lot of paste colour is needed and this makes the paste soft and sticky.)

STAGE FOUR

7 **Making the wings** Transfer the cake to the board. Roll out half of the red modelling paste between 2.5mm (⅛in) spacers. Cut one edge straight and position from the head over the top of the ladybird's back and down to the lower edge. Position it at an angle so that the wing appears slightly open. Ease in the fullness and cut the wing to size. Repeat on the other side.

b *Remove the crusts from both cakes and cut and smooth them into shape.*

c *Cover the underside of the ladybird with a strip of rolled out black sugarpaste.*

d *Use a circle cutter to make the spots from black modelling paste.*

8 **Making the spots** Roll out some of the black modelling paste and cut out 3.5cm (1⅜in) circles. Attach the circles in position (see picture **d**) and then carefully smooth the cut edges by circling each with a finger.

9 **Making the feet** Roll six 2.5cm (1in) balls of black modelling paste then roll each into a 5cm (2in) cone and attach in position around the base of the cake (see picture **e**).

10 **Forming the face** Roll a small amount of black modelling paste into a thin strand and glue onto the head in a 'U' shape to make the mouth. Add a tiny amount of red modelling paste to some of the white sugarpaste to make it pink. Thinly roll this out, cut two 2cm (¾in) circles and glue to the face at the corners of the mouth to make cheeks. For the eyes, roll a 1cm (½in) ball of white sugarpaste and cut it in half – this ensures each eye is the same size. Roll each half into a ball, elongate and flatten. Make smaller balls of black for pupils and even smaller white ones for light spots. Next, thinly roll strands of black modelling paste and cut to make eyelashes (see picture **f**). Glue in place.

11 **Making the bow** Thinly roll out the yellow modelling paste between spaces and cut into two 3cm (1¼in) wide strips. To form the ribbon tails, cut both ends of one strip at the same angle – this strip should be 10cm (4in) in length. For the loops, cut a second strip to a length of 18cm (7in). Mark the centre of this strip and bring the ends of the strip in to make the loops. Place the loops on top of the tail strip and slightly squeeze the centre together. Finish off the bow by wrapping a 1.5cm (⅝in) strip around the centre. Attach in place on the ladybird.

12 **Creating the antennae** Model two 1.5cm (⅝in) wide balls from black modelling paste. Make a hole in each with a dowel, place glue in the holes and position on top of the dried pastillage antennae. With a dowel, make two holes in the top of the ladybird's head and insert the antennae, adjusting as necessary (see picture **h**). Attach a ribbon around the board.

Use three strips of yellow modelling paste to create the ladybird's bow.

e *Model cones of black modelling paste for feet and place them in position.*

f *Make the ladybird's face from pink and white sugarpaste and black modelling paste.*

g *Attach the antennae by securing them into holes on top of the ladybird's head.*

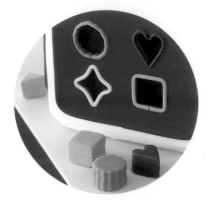

Shape Sorter

Which shape goes in which hole? Young children love playing with shape sorters and this cake will appeal to young minds as they learn about shapes, colours and how to tell the time. You can vary the colours and shapes to suit the birthday girl or boy.

CAKE AND DECORATION

8 egg madeira cake baked in
2 x 15cm (6in) square tins
(see page 11)

25cm (10in) square cake board

2kg (4lb 6oz) sugarpaste
(rolled fondant)

Yellow, orange, green, purple,
red, blue and black paste
food colours

One quantity of buttercream

Gum tragacanth

White vegetable fat (shortening)

Sugar glue

105cm (40in) red ribbon

EQUIPMENT

Carving knives

Waxed paper

Rolling pin

5mm (¼in) spacers
(e.g. strip wood from DIY stores)

Smoothers

Tilting turntable (optional)

Non-stick work board

2.5mm (⅛in) spacers
(e.g. skewers or thick cardboard)

Circle cutter

Set square

Shape cutters or templates

Sugar shaper (optional)

STAGE ONE

 1 **Covering the board** Colour 700g (1lb 7oz) of sugarpaste (rolled fondant) a rich yellow. Roll it out and cover the board. Keep the trimmings. Place to one side to dry.

STAGE TWO

 2 **Carving the cake** Level the cakes and cut away the crusts. Spread a thin layer of buttercream over the top of one cake and stack the other on top. Take a small carving knife and curve all the edges (see picture **a**). Place the cake on waxed paper.

3 **Covering the sides of the cake** Spread a thin layer of buttercream over the cake to stick the sugarpaste. Roll out the white sugarpaste between 5mm (¼in) spacers, and cut into a 65cm (25in) long and 18cm (7in) wide strip. Carefully roll up the paste like a bandage and position it against the side of the cake. Next, unroll the paste around the cake (see picture **b**) and rub the join closed.

 4 **Covering the top of the cake** Ease the sugarpaste over the top edge of the cake and cut a square of white sugarpaste to fit the top. Place the square of sugarpaste in position and blend the joins closed.

a Stack the cakes and carefully round all the edges using a small carving knife.

b Spread the cake with buttercream and unroll the white sugarpaste around the cake.

Use the smoothers to create a flat finish to the sides and top of the cake but do not worry too much about any marks because these will be covered later. Finally, polish all the edges of the cube with the palm of your hand and leave to dry thoroughly.

5 **Mixing the pastes** Add 2.5ml (½ teaspoon) gum tragacanth to 100g (3½oz) of the yellow trimmings. Place 50g (2oz) to one side and colour the other 50g (2oz) orange. Then, add 7.5ml (1½ teaspoons) gum tragacanth to 350g (12 oz) of the white sugarpaste trimmings to make modelling paste. Colour it as follows: 75g (3oz) green, 50g (2oz) purple, 150g (5oz) red, 50g (2oz) blue and 25g (1oz) black. Allow the gum to take effect. You will feel the difference in the consistency after a few hours, but it is best if you can leave it overnight if possible.

STAGE THREE

6 **Preparing the side panels** Place the cake on a tilting turntable or, alternatively, prop the cake on to one side. Smear your work board with white vegetable fat (shortening) to prevent the paste from sticking, and knead the red modelling paste, adding a little white vegetable fat to soften it if necessary. Roll out some of the red modelling paste between the 2.5mm (⅛in) spacers (see picture).

7 **Attaching the panels** Measure the side dimensions of your cake and cut out a square or rectangle from the red modelling paste 5cm (2in) shorter than your measurements. Round the corners by cutting away the paste with the circle cutter. Glue the panel centrally to one side of the cake and use the set square to ensure that the sides are straight. Mark the position of the panel on the cake before gluing it in place. Repeat for the other sides and the top.

8 **Creating the shaped holes** Choose an assortment of shape cutters or make your own template shapes. Decide which cutters or templates you want to use on each side.

c Roll out the red modelling paste between spacers to make the side panels.

d Carefully press the shape cutters into the red paste and remove the cut-out pieces.

e Replace the cut-out shapes with black modelling paste shapes.

Begin to cut the shapes from the red modelling paste to reveal the white below (see picture). Roll out the black paste very thinly and replace each shape with a black one (see picture e).

9 **Edging the holes** Soften some blue modelling paste by adding white vegetable fat and a drop or two of boiled water. Knead until malleable. Place the paste in the sugar shaper with the medium disc. Paint glue around the edge of one of the shapes, squeeze out a length from the sugar shaper and position the strip around the shape. Repeat for the other shapes (see picture f), changing colour as desired.

10 **Edging the panels** Soften some red modelling paste and place in the sugar shaper with the large disc. Paint glue around the sides of a panel, then squeeze out a length of paste from the sugar shaper and wrap it around the edges of the panel. Repeat for the other panels.

11 **Making the clock** Roll out the yellow modelling paste between 2.5mm (⅛in) spacers, cut out a 10cm (4in) circle and glue it to the top of the cake. Cut clock hands from thinly rolled blue modelling paste and glue them in position. Roll small blue and green balls and attach these to the clock face to mark the hours. Finally, place some softened green modelling paste in the sugar shaper with the medium sized round disc and squeeze out a length to go around the clock face.

12 **Making the shapes** Take the blue modelling paste and roll it out to a thickness of 1cm (½in). Cut two triangles (see picture g) and place one on top of the other to create a 2cm (¾in) deep shape. Repeat for the other shapes and colours until you have enough to scatter over the board (see picture h).

13 **Adding the finishing touches** Transfer the finished cake to the board and scatter the shapes around it. Finally, attach a ribbon around the edge of the board using non-toxic glue.

TIPS

★ If you do not have a sugar shaper do not worry – roll sausages of paste by hand. (A sugar shaper just saves time.)

★ If the circle for your clock distorts, you may find it easier to place the yellow paste on top of the cake and cut out the clock face in situ.

f Use a sugar shaper to make the edging for the red side panels and shape holes.

g Cut out two triangles before stacking them together to make a chunky shape.

h Make a selection of shapes in colours of your choice to scatter around the board.

Bubbles the Fish

Goldfish are among the most popular pets. Their bright scales gleaming as they swim in and out of the weeds in the pond. Bubbles is a very cheery fish and he can be adapted easily – by changing the colours, you can achieve many different effects.

CAKE AND DECORATION

6 egg madeira cake baked in a 3 litre/6 pint/15 cup ovenproof bowl (see page 11)

35.5cm (14in) round cake board

1.8kg (4lb) sugarpaste (rolled fondant)

Blue, orange, red and yellow paste food colours

Gum tragacanth

Half quantity of buttercream

White vegetable fat (shortening)

Sugar glue

Piping gel

1.2m (47in) blue ribbon

EQUIPMENT

Waxed paper

Fish templates (see page 94)

Non-stick work board

2mm (1/16 in) spacers (e.g. thick cardboard)

Cutting wheel (optional)

Sugar shaper

Scriber/craft knife

Circle cutters:
4cm (1½in), 2.5cm (1in) and 2cm (¾in) for the eye
3.5cm (1⅜in) for the scales

Smoother

Paintbrush

STAGE ONE

 Covering the board Colour 1kg (2lb 4oz) of sugarpaste (rolled fondant) a rich blue. Roll it out and use it to cover the board, trimming the sugarpaste flush with the edge. Place to one side to dry.

 Colouring the sugarpaste Colour 600g (1lb 5oz) of sugarpaste a deep orange. This is likely to make the paste quite sticky so, to overcome the problem, add 5ml (1 teaspoon) gum tragacanth to the coloured paste and leave for a few hours. This will make the paste firmer and easier to handle.

STAGE TWO

 Covering the cake Level the bowl-shaped cake, remove the crust and then place it on waxed paper (see picture ⓐ). Spread a thin layer of buttercream over the cake to help stick the sugarpaste. Roll out the deep orange sugarpaste and cover the cake. Carefully trim around the base, keeping the trimmings to one side, and leave to dry.

Making modelling paste Add 5ml (1 teaspoon) gum tragacanth to 200g (7oz) of the deep orange trimming. Place 100g (3½oz) to one side and colour 50g (2oz) a mid red and 50g (2oz) deep red. Next, add 5ml (1 teaspoon) gum tragacanth to the remaining 200g (7oz) white sugarpaste.

ⓐ *Once the cake has cooled, prepare it by levelling the base and removing the crust.*

ⓑ *Cut around the template to make the tail fins from rolled-out orange modelling paste.*

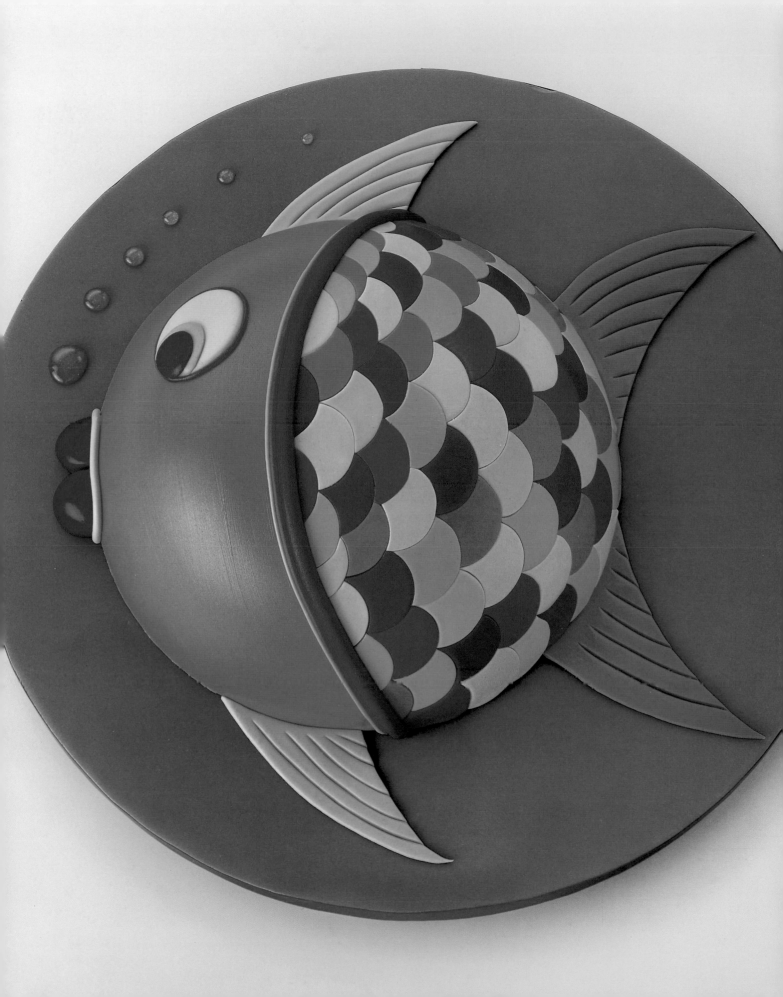

Colour 100g (3½oz) rich yellow, 50g (2oz) yellow-orange and 50g (2oz) pale orange. Add a further pinch or two of gum to the darker colours – these are the ones you have added more paste colour to. Leave the gum to take effect (preferably overnight) and then check that all the pastes are firm enough to be rolled thinly. Add more gum if necessary or, if the paste has become too stiff, add a little white vegetable fat (shortening) and a drop of cooled boiled water. Knead well to soften.

STAGE THREE

5 **Making the fins and tail** Transfer the cake to the board. Trace the templates onto waxed paper or card and cut them out. Smear white vegetable fat onto a non-stick work board and roll out some of the rich yellow modelling paste between the spacers. Place the fin templates on top of the paste, carefully cut the fins out and position on the board. Make the tail fins in the same way using the deep orange modelling paste (see picture **b**, page 80). Next, take a wheeled cutting tool and texture the fins and tail by carefully rolling the tool through the modelling paste (see picture **c**).

6 **Making the lips** Take the deep red modelling paste and roll a 2cm (¾in) wide ball and another slightly smaller ball. Place the balls at the front of the fish with the smaller ball on top. Then, with a finger, ease the paste towards the body of the fish to eliminate the gap between the lips and the body. Soften some of the rich yellow paste by adding white vegetable fat and a few drops of boiled water and place in a sugar shaper together with the medium round disc. Squeeze out a length of paste, place over the join between the lips and body and trim to size (see picture **d**). Note: If you do not have a sugar shaper, this edging strip can be rolled easily by hand.

7 **Marking the scale end curve** Squeeze out another length of paste from the sugar shaper and place over the body of the fish in a curve to mark where the scales will finish. With a scriber or craft knife, use the strip of paste as a guide and then mark the curve onto the body of the fish. Carefully remove the yellow paste.

c Use a cutting wheel to add the textured lines to the fish's fins and tail.

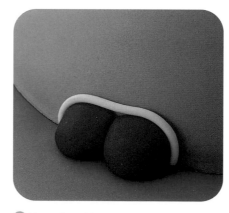

d The yellow strip defines the lips and hides the join between them and the fish's face.

e Cut yellow, orange and red circles and a strip of red paste to make up the eye.

8 Making the eye Roll out some deep yellow modelling paste and cut out a 4cm (1½in) circle. Next, cut a 2.5cm (1in) and a 2cm (¾in) circle from the yellow-orange and deep red modelling pastes respectively. Then, soften some mid red modelling paste by adding white vegetable fat and boiled water and place in a sugar shaper with the small round disc. Squeeze out a length of paste. You now have all the pieces to form the eye (see picture). Place the yellow-orange and red circles on top of the deep yellow circle and attach to the fish, smoothing the cut edges with a finger to give curved edges. Attach the strip of red paste around the eye, cut to size and blend the join.

9 Making the scales Roll out the yellow-orange modelling paste between the spacers. Cut a 3.5cm (1⅜in) circle and stick it to the body between the tail fins. Take the circle cutter and remove two sections of the circle to give a scale shape. Cut two circles from different colours of modelling paste and place in the cut away sections of the first scale. Then, cut scales to fit along side the first scale. Smooth the scales flat with a smoother then continue making and attaching scales (see pictures f and g) until the scales cover the body of the fish up to the scribed curve.

10 Making the trimming Place some softened modelling paste together with the large round disc in the sugar shaper and squeeze out a length. Attach to the edge of the scales. Repeat with the smaller discs and two other colours and attach these lengths also.

11 Adding the bubbles Place some piping gel in a bowl over a simmering pan of water until the gel has softened and is lump-free. Remove from the heat. Dip a paintbrush into the heated gel and carefully touch the board to create a water bubble. Repeat as desired.

12 Adding the finishing touches To add shine, apply a thin layer of white vegetable fat over the fish with a paintbrush (see picture h). Then, attach the ribbon around the edge of the board with non-toxic glue.

TIP
★ You will need a lot of paste colour to achieve a good depth of colour.

f Use the circle cutter to cut two sections of scale away at a time. Add scales as before.

g Add scales into the spaces that have been cut away by the circle cutter.

h Use a paintbrush to add a layer of white fat over the fish to create a shiny finish.

Fighter Jet

In spite of its tremendous power and speed, the fighter jet is an amazingly graceful machine. This cake is set high above the clouds as the jet makes its way back to base. You can easily adapt the decoration of the plane's wings and tail to suit the cake's recipient.

CAKE AND DECORATION

6 egg 20cm (8in) round madeira cake (see page 11)

33cm (13in) round cake board

2.25kg (5lb) sugarpaste (rolled fondant)

White, blue, black, olive green and red paste food colours

Gum tragacanth

125g (4½oz) pastillage

White vegetable fat (shortening)

Sugar glue

Half quantity of buttercream

100cm (40in) pale blue ribbon

EQUIPMENT

Jet templates (see page 91)

Waxed paper

Non-stick work board

2mm (¹⁄₁₆in) spacers (e.g. card)

Craft knife/cutting wheel

Foam or kitchen paper

Small metal file

Smoother

Scissors

Foam pieces

Carving knife

Sugar shaper (optional)

Star cutter

Paintbrush

STAGE ONE

1 **Covering the board** Colour 900g (2lb) sugarpaste (rolled fondant) a light blue-green by adding blue and a touch of olive green paste food colour. Cover the board and leave to dry.

2 **Mixing the pastes** Add 5ml (1 teaspoon) gum tragacanth to 225g (8oz) white sugarpaste to make modelling paste. Remove 15g (½oz) and colour it red, then colour the rest a grey-green by adding small amounts of black and olive green paste food colour. Colour the pastillage to match the modelling paste. (Note: the pastillage will dry a slightly lighter colour.)

3 **Making the wings and tail fins** Trace templates 1–3 onto waxed paper or card. Smear white vegetable fat (shortening) onto the non-stick work board and roll out the pastillage to a thickness of 2mm (¹⁄₁₆in) using spacers. Place template 1 on top of the paste and carefully cut around it – a cutting wheel is ideal for this as it does not drag the paste. Transfer the pastillage shape to a flat porous surface, such as foam or kitchen paper. Cut two pastillage shapes for each of the remaining templates, then place these with the first piece and allow to dry thoroughly (see picture).

a Using the templates, cut out the jet, wings and tail fin shapes from the pastillage.

b Slot the jet-shaped pastillage piece into the slot in the underside of the jet's nose.

Short cuts

⏱ Have one big cloud rather than a few smaller ones.

⏱ Leave out the paint stippling stage for the board.

⏱ Simplify the jet detail.

⏱ Use a toy jet or paper aeroplane instead of making your own jet.

STAGE TWO

4 **Making the body of the jet** If necessary, gently file each piece of pastillage to remove any rough edges. Take 100g (3½oz) of the grey-green modelling paste and, following the body template, roll the paste into the body shape of the jet using a smoother to get an even finish. Place the underside of the jet on a flat surface to flatten it slightly, then turn the shape onto its side and cut a slit in the underside. Spread sugar glue onto the cut surfaces and slot the jet-shaped pastillage piece, nose end first, into the body and press closed (see picture **b**).

5 **Making the tail** Make a 5cm (2in) long tapered sausage, tapering from 2cm (¾in) down to 1cm (½in). With a pair of scissors, make two 2cm (¾in) long cuts into the paste at right angles to each other at the narrower end of the sausage. At the wider end make a 2.5cm (1in) long cut through the paste, spread sugar glue onto the cut surfaces and slot onto the pastillage shape so that it is positioned on the back end of the jet's body.

6 **Making the engines** Make two 7.5cm (3in) long, 2 cm (¾in) wide tapered sausages to form the engine shapes. Then, with a craft knife, cut a number of 1cm (½in) lines around the widest ends. Next, make a 5.5cm (2¼in) cut through the narrow end of each engine (see picture **c**), spread the cut surfaces with glue and slot onto the pastillage either side of the tail. Attach the lower fins to the lower edge of each engine and glue the upper fins in place, supporting each in position with foam whilst the glue dries (see picture **d**).

STAGE THREE

7 **Carving the cake** Remove the crust from the cake and divide it roughly into three or four pieces. Shape each section into a cloud by rounding and shaping the cut edges (see picture **e**). There is no precision required here. Use the trimmings to make more clouds if you wish.

c *Cut a slot in the end of each engine piece so that you can attach them to the pastillage.*

d *Support the tail fins in position with small pieces of foam until everything is dry.*

e *Carve the cake into roughly shaped pieces to represent the clouds.*

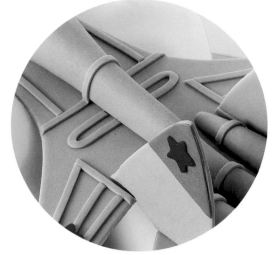

 Covering the cake Place the cakes on waxed paper and cover with a thin layer of buttercream. Next, cover each piece of cake with white sugarpaste, smooth the paste and trim away the excess from around the base.

 Adding the jet detail Make thin strips of grey modelling paste to decorate the jet by cutting them by hand. Alternatively, place some softened paste in a sugar shaper together with the small ribbon disc and squeeze out strips of paste to the approximate lengths you require. Referring to the photograph, paint lines of glue onto the jet where the strips are to be positioned. Arrange the strips over the glue and cut them to size with a craft knife (see picture f).

 Adding the trim Darken 25g (1oz) grey modelling paste by adding some black paste colour to it. Roll it out very thinly and use to trim the fins, wing tips and nose. Then, add red stars cut from thinly rolled red modelling paste to the wings and fins.

11 **Making the cockpit** Add black colour to a little of the grey modelling paste to make a black paste. Position it on top of the jet, to form the cockpit. Smooth the paste into shape with your fingers and cut away the excess.

STAGE FOUR

12 **Arranging the cake** Place the covered cloud cakes onto the board and secure in position. Place some undiluted white paste food colour on a paintbrush and paint and stipple the board randomly around the clouds (see picture g). Decide on the position of the jet and glue in place (see picture h). To finish the cake, attach your chosen ribbon around the edge of the board.

TIP

★ *If using a sugar shaper, soften the modelling paste first by adding some white vegetable fat and a few drops of boiled water and knead until malleable (rather like chewing gum).*

f *Attach strips of grey modelling paste for the jet detail. Trim to size with a craft knife.*

g *Stipple diluted white paste food colour onto the board around the clouds.*

h *Carefully glue the jet in position on top of the clouds.*

Smiley Face

Smile and the world smiles with you! This cheerful sunny cake will brighten up anyone's day. You can change the colour combinations as required but aim for bright and warm tones on this simple cake to make sure you bring a smile to everyone's face.

CAKE AND DECORATION

6 egg madeira cake baked in a 3 litre/6 pint/15 cup ovenproof bowl (see page 11)

28cm (11in) square cake board

1.1kg (2lb 7oz) sugarpaste (rolled fondant)

Gum tragacanth

Purple, black, yellow, orange and red paste food colours

Half quantity of buttercream

Clear spirit, such as gin or vodka

Sugar glue

White vegetable fat (shortening)

1.2m (48in) purple ribbon

EQUIPMENT

Waxed paper

2mm (¹⁄₁₆in) spacers (e.g. barbecue skewers)

20cm (8in) plate or cake tin

Paintbrushes

Natural sponge

Face template (see page 91)

Circle cutters:
5.5cm (2¹⁄₈in) for the cheeks
3.5cm (1³⁄₈in) for the pupil
1cm (³⁄₈in) for the light spot

Sugar shaper (optional)

STAGE ONE

 1 **Covering the board** Roll out 800g (1lb 12oz) of white sugarpaste (rolled fondant) and cover the board, trimming the sugarpaste flush with the edge. Place to one side to dry.

 2 **Mixing pastes** Add 2.5ml (½ teaspoon) gum tragacanth to 100g (3½oz) of sugarpaste to make modelling paste and colour 50g (2oz) purple and 25g (1oz) black. Colour the remaining sugarpaste yellow.

STAGE TWO

 3 **Covering the cake** Level the bowl-shaped cake, remove the crust (see picture **a**) and place on waxed paper. Apply a layer of buttercream. Roll out the yellow sugarpaste and cover the cake. Trim and leave to dry.

 4 **Colouring the board** Roll out the purple modelling paste between 2mm (¹⁄₁₆in) spacers and cut four 5mm (¼in) wide strips. Attach each strip to the edge of the board and mitre the corners where they join. Mark a 20cm (8in) circle on the board by placing a plate or cake tin in position and scribing around it. Dilute some orange, red and purple paste colours with a little clear spirit and, using a large paintbrush, roughly paint orange around the circle. Follow this with a red circle (see picture **b**) then fill in the corners with purple.

a *Once the cake has cooled, level the base and remove all of the crusts.*

b *Use a large flat-headed paintbrush to paint around the marked circle.*

Short cuts

⏱ Omit one or all of the painting stages.

⏱ Cover the board with suitable wrapping paper and place the cake on a 20cm (8in) circle of waxed paper to protect its underside before placing it on the board.

Next, very carefully pour clear spirit or cooled boiled water over the painted surface (see picture). Use a paintbrush to encourage the liquid into the corners. You will find that, as the liquid melts the surface of the paste, the colours merge. Be patient, it takes a minute or two to work. Leave for a few hours until the sugarpaste surface of the board is quite syrupy. Take a fine paintbrush and pull the colour from the edge of the board towards the centre (see picture d). Repeat until you have a radial pattern. Leave to dry in a warm place.

STAGE THREE

5 **Painting the cake** Dilute some dark orange, mid orange and yellow paste colours with clear spirit. Take a damp natural sponge, dip it into the dark orange colour and, starting at the lower edge of the cake, press the sponge around the cake. Change to the mid orange colour and sponge above and partially over the dark orange. As you move towards the centre of the cake, finish off with yellow (see picture e). Leave to dry.

STAGE FOUR

6 **Making the face** Transfer the cake to the board. Make an eye template, thinly roll out the white modelling paste and cut out two ovals. Using sugar glue, stick these to the face. Cut two pupils from black modelling paste using a 3.5cm (1⅜in) circle cutter and cut two light spots from white modelling paste using a 1cm (⅜in) circle cutter. Place in position and round the edges with your finger. For the eyebrows, soften some yellow sugarpaste by adding white fat and a drop of water and place in a sugar shaper with the medium round disc. Squeeze out two lengths and position as eyebrows. For the nose, make a 2cm (¾in) ball from the yellow sugarpaste, flatten and stick to the face. For the mouth, colour some modelling paste red, soften it and place in the sugar shaper. Squeeze it into a smile directly onto the cake. For the cheeks, cut two 5.5cm (2⅛in) circles from yellow sugarpaste, stick them in place and soften the edges.

7 **Adding the final touches** Use a paintbrush to stipple over the cheeks, nose and eyebrows with the diluted orange and yellow paste colours. Finally, attach a ribbon around the board.

TIPS

★ If you have not tried flood painting before, experiment on some spare sugarpaste. I really like this technique because some wonderful effects can be created.

★ For speed and uniformity, a sugar shaper is used for the mouth and eyebrows. However, these pieces could easily be rolled by hand.

c To encourage the colours to merge, pour a little clear spirit onto the painted surface.

d Once the surface has become syrupy, carefully brush the colours to the centre.

e Paint the surface of the cake using a sponge and diluted paste food colours.

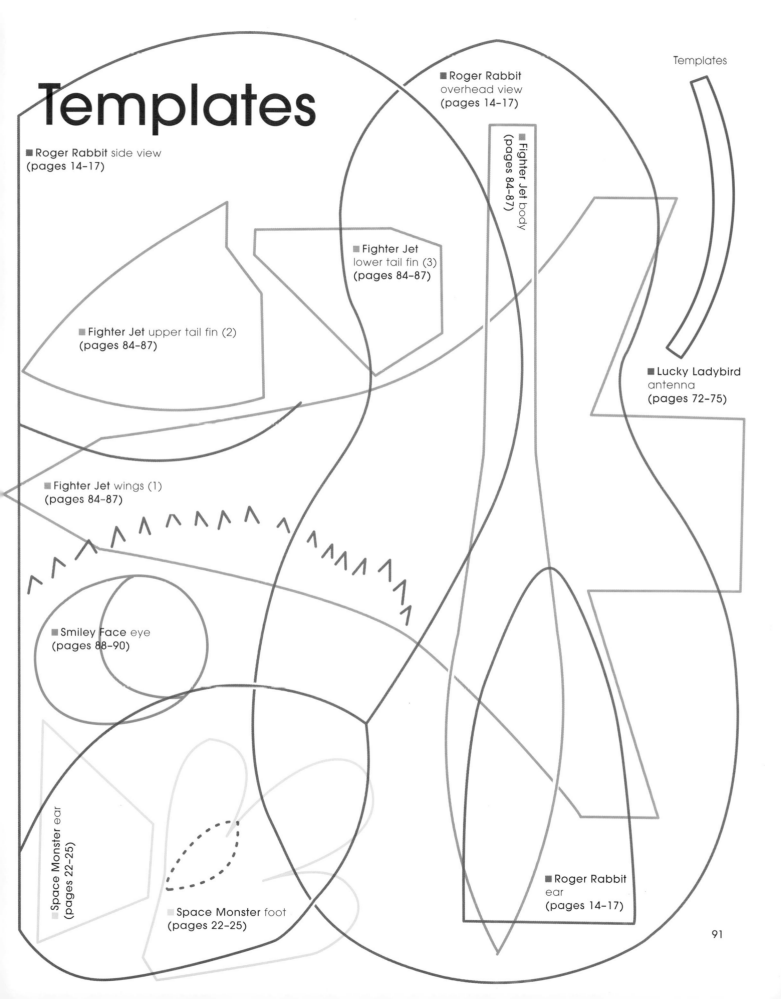

Templates

■ **Roger Rabbit** side view
(pages 14–17)

■ **Roger Rabbit**
overhead view
(pages 14–17)

■ **Fighter Jet** body
(pages 84–87)

■ **Fighter Jet**
lower tail fin (3)
(pages 84–87)

■ **Fighter Jet** upper tail fin (2)
(pages 84–87)

■ **Lucky Ladybird**
antenna
(pages 72–75)

■ **Fighter Jet** wings (1)
(pages 84–87)

■ **Smiley Face** eye
(pages 88–90)

■ **Space Monster** ear
(pages 22–25)

■ **Space Monster** foot
(pages 22–25)

■ **Roger Rabbit**
ear
(pages 14–17)

91

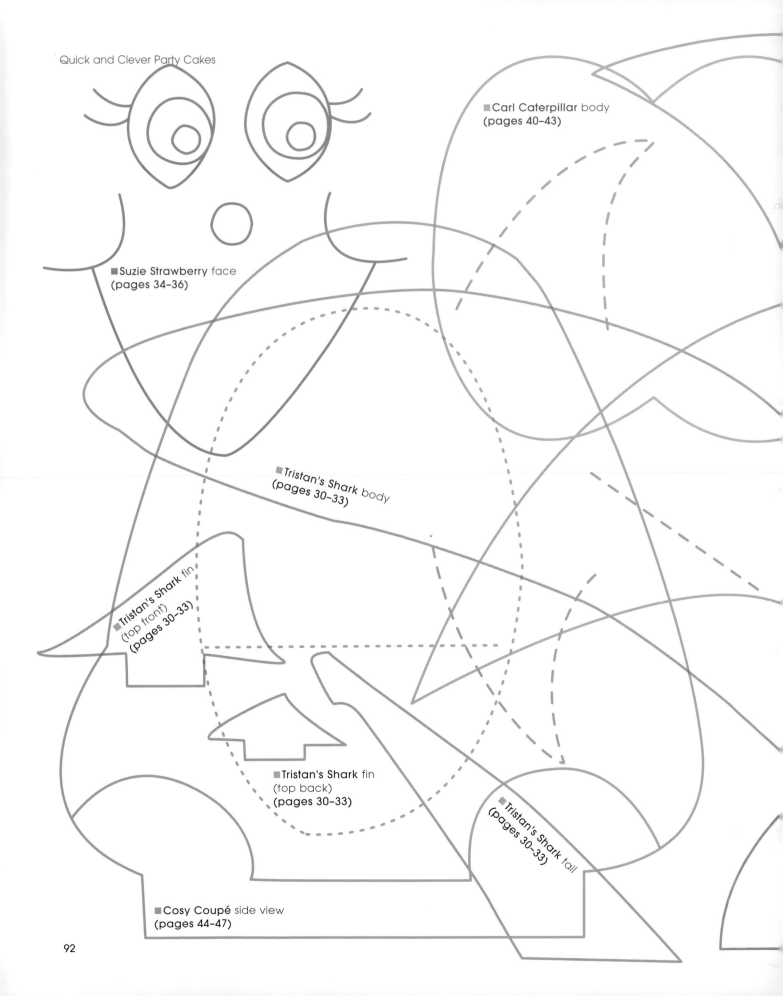

■Carl Caterpillar body
(pages 40–43)

■Suzie Strawberry face
(pages 34–36)

■Tristan's Shark body
(pages 30–33)

■Tristan's Shark fin
(top front)
(pages 30–33)

■Tristan's Shark fin
(top back)
(pages 30–33)

■Tristan's Shark tail
(pages 30–33)

■Cosy Coupé side view
(pages 44–47)

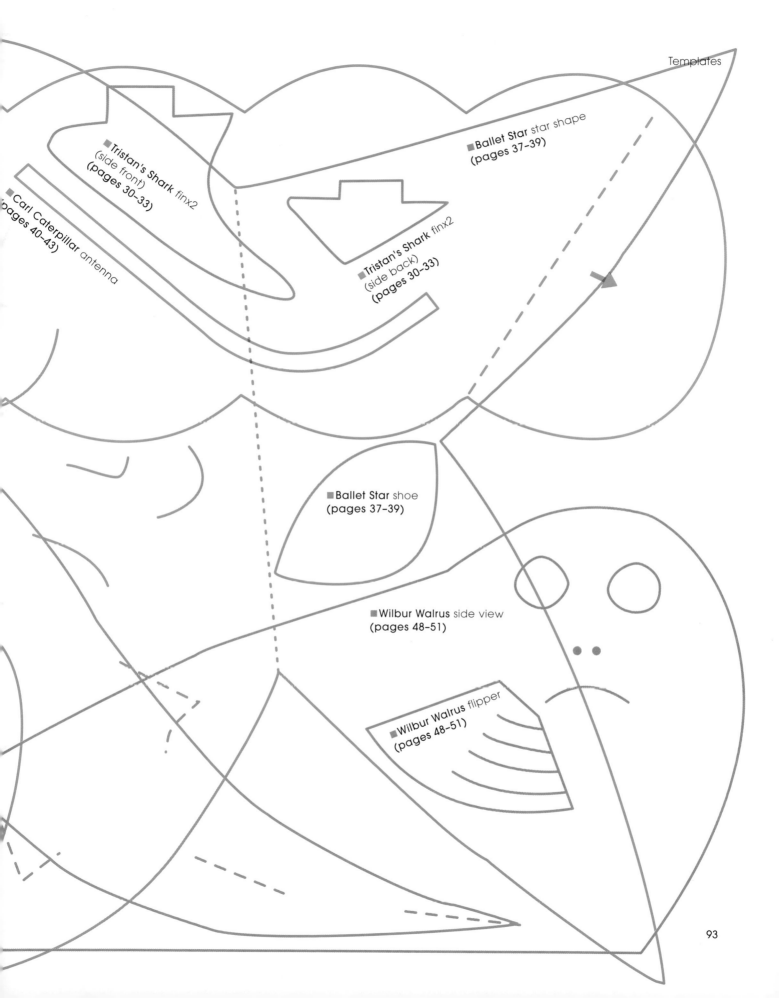

■Tristan's Shark finx2
(side front)
(pages 30–33)

■Ballet Star star shape
(pages 37–39)

■Carl Caterpillar antenna
(pages 40–43)

■Tristan's Shark finx2
(side back)
(pages 30–33)

■Ballet Star shoe
(pages 37–39)

■Wilbur Walrus side view
(pages 48–51)

■Wilbur Walrus flipper
(pages 48–51)

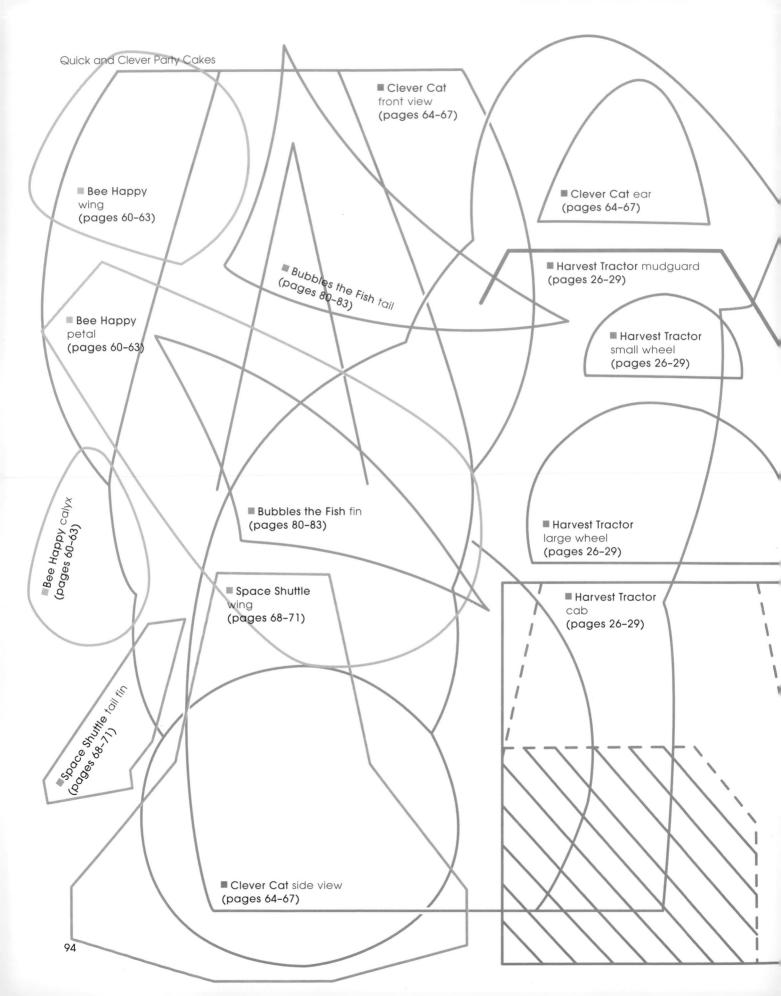

■ Bee Happy
wing
(pages 60–63)

■ Clever Cat
front view
(pages 64–67)

■ Clever Cat ear
(pages 64–67)

■ Bee Happy
petal
(pages 60–63)

■ Bubbles the Fish tail
(pages 80–83)

■ Harvest Tractor mudguard
(pages 26–29)

■ Harvest Tractor
small wheel
(pages 26–29)

Bee Happy calyx
(pages 60–63)

■ Bubbles the Fish fin
(pages 80–83)

■ Harvest Tractor
large wheel
(pages 26–29)

■ Space Shuttle
wing
(pages 68–71)

■ Harvest Tractor
cab
(pages 26–29)

Space Shuttle tail fin
(pages 68–71)

■ Clever Cat side view
(pages 64–67)

Acknowledgements

I would like to thank my family for putting up with the piles of boxes that seemed to rapidly multiply and take over our living room – children, your friends will no longer think we are moving house!; Zack and Ceri for allowing their rabbit Jet to model for me; Sofi for lending me her cosy coupé; Julia for the use of her work board – I will get my own I promise; and Ceinwen, Rita, Jinc and Julia for looking after my children when I was needed elsewhere.

lindysmith@lineone.net

www.lindyscakes.co.uk

Suppliers (in alphabetical order)

Alan Silverwood Ltd
(Manufacturer of multisized cake pan and spherical moulds/ball tins)
Ledsam House
Ledsam Street
Birmingham B16 8DN
Tel: +44 (0)121 454 3571
(for stockists and brochure)

B&D Manufacturing Ltd
(Manufacturer of sugar shapers)
15 Albert Road
Aldershot
Hampshire, GU11 1SZ
Tel: +44 (0)1252 341553

Ceefor Cakes
(Supplier of strong cake boxes)
15 Nelson Road
Leighton Buzzard
Bedfordshire, LU7 8EE
Tel: +44 (0)12525 375237
email: ceefor.cakes@virgin.net

Culpitt /Cake Art
(Trade supplier)
Jubilee Industrial Estate
Ashington
Northumberland, NE63 8UQ
Tel: +44 (0)1670 814 545
Customer Service Line:
+44 (0)1670 842800
www.culpitt.com

FMM Sugarcraft (FMM)
(Manufacturer of zigzag cutter)
Unit 5, Kings Park Industrial Estate
Primrose Hill
Kings Langley
Hertfordshire, WD4 8ST
Tel: +44 (0)1923 268699
email: clements@f-m-m. demon.co.uk

Guy, Paul & Co. Ltd
(trade supplier)
Unit B4 Foundry Way
Little End Road
Eaton Socon
Cambs, PE19 3JH
Tel: +44 (0)1480 472545
email: sukhi@guypaul.co.uk
www.guypaul.co.uk

Holly Products (HP)
(Supplier of textured rolling pins)
Holly Cottage
Hassall Green
Sandbach
Cheshire, CW11 4YA
Tel: +44 (0)1270 761403
email: june.twelves@u.genie.co.uk
www.hollyproducts.co.uk

Orchard Products (OP)
(Supplier of unbreakable gel)
51 Hallyburton Road
Hove
East Sussex, BN3 7GP
Tel: +44 (0)800 9158226
email: gsfashby@aol.com

Patchwork Cutters (PC)
(Supplier of mini quilting embosser)
3 Raines Close
Greasby
Wirral
Merseyside, CH49 2QB
Tel: +44 (0)151 678 5053

Piece of Cake
(Mail order decorating supplies)
18–20 Upper High Street
Thame
Oxfordshire, OX9 3EX
Tel: +44 (0)1844 213428
email:sales@pieceofcakethame.co.uk
www.apieceofcakethame.co.uk

PME Sugarcraft (PME)
(Manufacturer of cutting wheels)
Brember Road
South Harrow, HA2 8UN
Tel: +44 (0)20 8864 0888
email: enquiry@pmeltd.co.uk
www.pmeltd.co.uk

Renshaw Scott Ltd
(Manufacturer of Regalice sugarpaste used in this book)
Crown Street
Liverpool, L8 7RF
Tel: +44 (0)1555 770711
email: info@renshawscott.co.uk
www.renshawscott.co.uk

Squires Kitchen (SK)
(Manufacturer and supplier of edible gold dust)
Squires House
3 Waverley Lane
Farnham
Surrey, GU9 8BB
Tel: +44 (0)1252 711749
email: squires@squires-group.co.uk
www.squires-group.co.uk
www.squires-shop.com

NON-UK

Beryl's Cake Decorating & Pastry Supplies
PO Box 1584
N. Springfield, United States
Tel: +1 800 488 2749

The Cake Decorators School of Australia
Shop 7, Port Phillip Arcade
232 Flinders Street
Melbourne
Victoria 3000
Australia
Tel: +61 (0)3 9654 5335
Fax: +61 (0)3 9654 5818

Cupid's Cake Decorations
2/90 Belford Street
Broadmeadow
New South Wales 2292
Australia
Tel: +61 (0)2 4962 1884
Fax: +61 (0)2 4961 6594

Suzy Q Cake Decorating Centre
Shop 4, 372 Keilor Road
Niddrie
Victoria, 3042
Australia
Tel: +61 (0)3 9379 2275

Ediciones Ballina Codai S.A.
Avda Cordoba 2415
1st Floor
C1120Aag
Buenos Aires
Argentina
Tel: +5411 4962 5381
Fax: +5411 4963 3751

First published in 2002 by Murdoch Books UK Ltd
Merehurst is an imprint of Murdoch Books UK Ltd
Copyright © 2002 Murdoch Books UK Ltd

ISBN 1 85391 830 X
A catalogue record of this book is available from the British Library.

Text copyright © Lindy Smith 2002
Lindy Smith has asserted her right under the Copyright, Designs and Patents Act, 1988, to be identified as Author of this work.

Commissioning Editor Barbara Croxford
Managing Editor Anna Osborn
Design Manager Helen Taylor
Photography Martin Brigdale
Design and Editorial Studio Cactus

CEO Robert Oerton
Publisher Catie Ziller
Production Manager Lucy Byrne
International Sales Director Kevin Lagden

Colour separation by Colourscan, Singapore
Printed by Giunti Industrie Grafiche

Murdoch Books UK Ltd
Ferry House
51–57 Lacy Road
Putney
London SW15 1PR
United Kingdom
Tel: +44 (0)20 8355 1480
Fax: +44 (0)20 8355 1499
Murdoch Books UK Ltd is a subsidiary of Murdoch Magazines Pty Ltd

UK Distribution
Macmillan Distribution Ltd
Houndmills, Brunell Road
Basingstoke, Hampshire RG21 6XS
United Kingdom
Tel: +44 (0)1256 302707
Fax: +44 (0)1256 351437
http://www.macmillan-mdl.co.uk

Murdoch Books ®
GPO Box1203, Sydney
NSW 1045, Australia
Tel: +61 (0)2 4352 7025
Fax: +61 (0)2 4352 7026
Murdoch Books® is a trademark of Murdoch Magazines Pty Ltd

Index